Be the Light, Become the Lighthouse

Book 1: SHINE

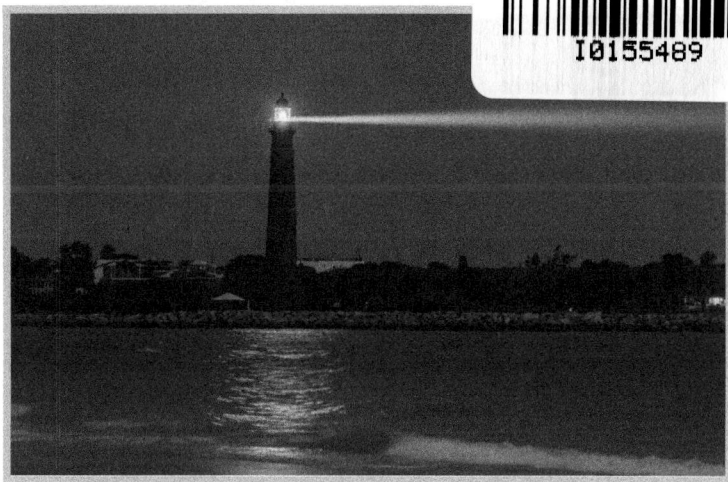

By: Pamela Gullotti

Copyright Disclaimer

First Edition, 2025
Paperback ISBN: 978-1-970987-01-0
Hardcover ISBN: 978-1-970987-03-4
Large Print ISBN: 978-1-970987-04-1
EBook/Kindle ISBN: 978-1-970987-02-7
Revised Edition, 2026
Paperback ISBN: 978-1-970987-00-3

Printed by Amazon KDP

The Chapters of My Spiritual Journey

Dedication

To my personal constellation, without whom this Lighthouse would just be a flashlight in the dark:

To my Earth — Grandfather Tony, Father Paul (Capricorns), and Grandmother Mary (Taurus): Thank you for the stubborn grit, the tough love, and the solid ground. You taught me that you can't build a Lighthouse on a wish; you need a rock.

To my Water — Stepmother Sharon (Cancer), Sister Paige, and my Son, A.J. Jr. (Scorpios): Thank you for the depth, the sanctuary, and the intensity. You taught me how to swim in the deep end without drowning and how to love the parts of life others are afraid to touch.

To my Fire — Brothers Paul II and Patrick (Sagittarius), and Nephew Sebastian (Leo): Thank you for the sparks, the wild laughter, and the blunt arrows of truth. You taught me that even a spiritual journey shouldn't be taken *too* seriously.

And from your lone Air sign (Libra): Thank you for giving me the ground to stand on, the ocean to watch over, and the fire to tend. I finally realized that Air is the only thing that lets the Light shine through.

"Like a beacon in the night, your light inspires and guides others."

"The planet does not need more successful people. The planet desperately needs more peacemakers, healers, restorers, storytellers, and lovers of every kind."
— Dalai Lama

Introduction: The Choice to Stay

In the world of spiritual awakening, there is a seductive promise that many of us chase. It is the promise of Ascension—the idea that if we meditate enough, heal enough, and raise our vibration high enough, we will finally rise above the chaos of the human experience. We are taught to detach, to float, to leave the "heaviness" of the 3D world behind.

For years, as a Highly Sensitive Person (HSP) and an Empath, I clung to this promise. I felt battered by the storms of other people's emotions and the noise of modern life. I thought the goal of my awakening was to build a spaceship and escape.

But I discovered a profound flaw in this plan. We are not here to leave. We are here to Light Up.

Teachers like Eckhart Tolle speak beautifully of the "Power of Now," teaching us that presence ends suffering. But for those of us who feel deeply, who are wired to connect, the "Now" can often feel like a battlefield. We don't need to just "be present" with the chaos; we need a structure strong enough to withstand it.

We cannot simply "ascend" and leave our humanity behind. If we float away, we become untethered kites, lost in the ether, of no use to ourselves or the world we came to serve.

The true master does not escape the storm. The true master becomes the Lighthouse that stands within it.

My name is Pamela Gullotti. I am an educator, a librarian, and a lifelong feeler. For decades, I lived as an "unguarded" Lighthouse. I absorbed the pain of those around me, thinking my empathy was a curse, waiting for the day I would finally be "spiritual enough" to stop feeling it all.

But I realized that my sensitivity wasn't a weakness to be transcended; it was the fuel for my light. The problem wasn't the light; it was that I hadn't built the Tower to hold it.

Book 1: SHINE is the manual for the awakened soul who chooses to stay. It is the guide to building your internal foundation so you can stop absorbing the darkness and start radiating the light. It is the journey of transforming from an Anxious Empath—who drowns in the waves—into a Sovereign Lighthouse, who shines without burning out.

In these pages, we will not learn how to detach from the world. We will learn how to Anchor into our own truth so deeply that the world cannot move us.

- We will learn how to **filter** the noise of the world so we can hear our own soul.
- We will **reframe** our past trauma not as damage, but as the bedrock of our stability.
- We will **master** the art of internal boundaries, realizing that we must fill our own cup before we can pour into others.
- We will **release** the need to be "rescued" and learn how to become our own source of peace.

This book is the first step: **SHINE**. It is about doing the internal work to ensure your light is steady, strong, and yours.

But a Lighthouse does not shine for itself. A Lighthouse is built for a purpose: to guide ships. To connect the land to the sea.

That is why this journey continues.

In **Book 2: BUILD**, we will look outward. We will explore how to take this new, strong self and build healthy, grounded relationships. We will correct the ancient tragedy of **Astraea**—the goddess who left Earth because she couldn't bear the chaos—by learning how to build structures that allow us to stay.

In **Book 3: CONNECT**, we will bring it all together. We will answer the error of *The Alchemist*—who left love behind to find his treasure—by proving that the "Grand Unification" of 3D and 5D is the true treasure. We will learn to speak the language of the Bridge, connecting our spiritual wisdom with our human reality.

And finally, in **Book 4: THRIVE**, we will master the rhythm of the seasons. Like **Hades and Persephone**, we will learn how to honor the cycles of solitude and union, proving that two sovereign souls—one of the Light and one of the Deep—can build a kingdom that lasts.

But before we can build the bridge, before we can walk across it, and before we can thrive in the new world, we must first ensure we have a light strong enough to show the way.

The world doesn't need you to leave. It needs you to turn on.

It starts here. It starts with you. It starts with **SHINE**.

The Ocean Answers

"Within you, there is a stillness and a sanctuary to which you can retreat at any time and be yourself."

— Hermann Hesse

Journal Entry:

Eventually, we all have to end up somewhere in life. This is nowhere near where I thought I'd be right now. But I've always held a fragile belief that I am exactly where I need to be at any given time; that all my moments have been leading up to this and things could have gone no other way. I am clinging to that hope today, as I have been every day for the past month.

The gentle, melodic waves of the sea have the ability to tame even the most restless soul. There have been several times in my life when the sea has called out my name, a soft whisper beneath the chaos. But this time is different. This time, I called out to the sea. I came here frantically questioning my direction in life, shouting my attachments and my fears at the water, demanding immediate answers.

The ocean, however, never wavered. It softly, rhythmically, crashed its waves upon the shore, letting me know that even though my life felt unsettled, its reply is not a thing that could be rushed. The ocean did not shout back. It did not meet my chaos with more chaos. It firmly stood its ground, a steady, unshakeable presence. It was a beacon in my storm, reminding me that I didn't need to fight the waves, but simply keep my feet planted in the sand and let life crash around me.

Therefore, the answers didn't come with the crashing waves, but rose and fell with the tide. Sometimes, though, even the water gets angry. The waves crash ashore with a fierceness that takes your breath away. But this moment, my first true pause, was a time for calm, quiet reflection—a time to look back and recognize how far I have come and a time to figure out how to plan a path that keeps me moving forward.

The sea didn't tell me this in words. I knew what it was saying the moment I arrived on its sandy beach. I never knew how much I needed to feel the sun on my face, the ocean breeze in my hair, the sand between my toes, and the salty waves caressing my feet. I never knew how much I needed to simply let myself feel. My life was demanding change, and to do that, I had to feel the world around me. I needed to stop long enough to listen to my heart, something I haven't always been great at in my life. Things like this cause a variety of emotions to rise and fall, just as the changing tides.

Emotions are a tricky thing, especially when we are taught to push them away, to "rise above" them and become stronger in any situation we find ourselves in. But I was learning that this suppression was exactly how I ended up here, running back to the ocean. Running from a home that no longer felt like my own. I didn't think my life would change so dramatically from one seemingly tiny decision. I needed to escape the chaos and when I did, I found a sense of peace that had been missing for so long I had forgotten that peace existed at all.

But it wasn't the act of running away that sealed my path; it was the profound realization that I did not want to return. After abandoning that life, I finally began to feel like myself again. Not just the shell of a woman I didn't even recognize when I looked in the mirror, but the 'Truth' of who I was, beginning to resurface. I was relearning how to love life, and more importantly, relearning how to love myself.

Once in a while, we choose to go deeper into the ocean, past the waves breaking on the shoreline where the water begins to settle around us. If we venture out far enough, we are met with the stillness and vastness of our world. In these moments, we realize that finding true peace begins with learning to live in that silence, finally calming the mind and listening to the 'Truth' of the heartbeat inside of us. This is the "pause" where clarity is born. It is only then that we can make life-altering decisions.

Once we accept ourselves, wholly and completely, we can begin to see through the chaos. We begin the process of filtering out the noise and bringing our own thoughts into focus. This process is a difficult one, one that we constantly avoid. But, clarity is often overlooked. We would rather push away the silence, sometimes running frantically, because the noise of the chaos feels easier. However, it is only a temporary one. Eventually the chaos settles, the noise falls gently into night, and the quiet softness returns upon us. The silence is eternal, and it arrives whether we embrace it or not.

Standing on this beach, having run back to the ocean, hoping to find myself among the sand and shells, I realized this silence was the answer I was looking for. The answer was not in the waves beating against the shore, endlessly churning in their pursuit to free themselves from their Creator. It was in the calm, deep, loving depths of the sea. That is what my soul had come to seek.

I began to find myself in that simplicity. I have come to learn that I need more from my life. I crave the freedom that comes with the deep water, the ability to float wherever the breeze takes me, not being pushed or pulled by external forces, but simply being, just drifting slowly among the sea life. Perhaps, until now, I never noticed how much life flourishes out here in the calm, deep water. I used to think the waves were bringing life to the sandy shore. And while life can exist in the chaos of the constant churning of these rough waters, it thrives in the stillness and gentle calmness of the deep ocean.

I now know, in my heart, that the ocean's answer was spoken in that silence. It has already been *told to me. The real reason I am here is to let myself learn to accept that truth—and finally begin to create my own path and chart my own course through the ocean of life.*

Inspiration:

Your breakdown is a breakthrough. The moment you feel completely lost, shouting at the uncaring waves, is the very moment you have finally stopped, become present, and are truly ready to listen for a new answer. Chaos is the fertilizer for profound change.

Book 1: SHINE

The Ocean Answers

I share this entry because it marks the precise moment the noise finally stopped. That day on the beach wasn't just about looking at the water; it was about confronting the terrifying reality that my life, as I knew it, had to break in order to be rebuilt.

The contrast between the chaotic, crashing waves and the calm, deep ocean became the first anchor of my new life. It captured the raw, desperate feeling of outgrowing my own existence and demanding answers from the Universe.

If you are holding this book, you may be standing in that same storm right now. You may feel that life is crashing around you, pulling you under. But as the ocean taught me, the answer isn't found by fighting the waves. It is found by sinking beneath them.

Here are the insights the ocean gave me, and how you can use them to navigate your own tides.

Insights from the Journey:

- **Meet Chaos with Calm:** The greatest lesson from the ocean was that it did not meet chaos with more chaos. When your inner world is frantic, the solution is not to "figure it out" more frantically. The solution is to find a single, steady presence—like the ocean's rhythm—and anchor yourself to it.

- **The Pause IS the Path:** The entry describes this as "my first true pause." We often think the "pause" is a *delay* from finding the answer. This insight reveals that the pause *is* the answer. Clarity isn't found in the frantic search; it's born in the stillness that follows.

- **Allow Feeling to Fuel Change:** The realization of "I never knew how much I needed to simply let myself feel" is key. Suppressing emotion is what keeps us stuck. Allowing yourself to feel the pain, the fear, and the joy is what gives you the data and the energy to make a genuine change, rather than just an intellectual one.

- **The Answer is in the "Deep," Not the "Waves":** The churning waves are like the chattering, anxious mind—loud, chaotic, and repetitive. The "Truth" of the soul, the real answers, are found in the "calm, deep, loving depths" *beneath* the surface noise.

Actionable Steps for Your Own Journey:

If you feel like you are at a similar breaking point, here are steps you can take, inspired by this journey:

Book 1: SHINE

1. **Create a "Pattern Interrupt":** The author ran to the ocean. You may not need to do something so drastic, but you must change your physical environment. If you are stuck in chaos, get out. Go to a park, a library, a coffee shop, or anywhere that breaks your routine. A new environment is the first step to new thoughts.

2. **Practice the Sacred Pause:** The next time you feel overwhelmed and frantic, set a timer for three minutes. Do nothing but sit and breathe. Do not try to solve the problem. Your only job is to *not* meet your inner chaos with more chaos. Be the ocean.

3. **Get Out of Your Head and Into Your Body:** The author describes *feeling* the sun, sand, and water. When you are spinning, ground yourself by naming:

   - **5** things you can see.

   - **4** things you can physically feel (your feet on the floor, the fabric of your shirt).

   - **3** things you can hear.

   - **2** things you can smell.

- ○ **1** thing you can taste. This pulls you from the "waves" of your mind into the "truth" of the present moment.

4. **Seek the "Deep" Over the "Waves":** When you try to meditate or find quiet, don't fight your thoughts (the waves). Acknowledge them, and then let your focus sink *under* them, to the place of deep, silent awareness that is always there. Your soul's 'Truth' is waiting in that silence, not in the noise.

Positive Affirmation:

I release the need for loud answers and embrace the quiet stillness within. In this pause, I listen to my own heart and clearly see my path forward.

The Garden in the Concrete

"The most beautiful people we have known are those who have known defeat, known suffering, known struggle, known loss, and have found their way out of the depths. These persons have an appreciation, a sensitivity, and an understanding of life that fills them with compassion, gentleness, and a deep loving concern. Beautiful people do not just happen."

— Elisabeth Kübler-Ross

Journal Entry:

Someone just said, "you are the rose that grew out of the concrete," and I immediately started tearing up. I felt this phrase deeply in my heart and soul. But the truth is, I never wanted to be that rose. I never asked for this. All I have ever wanted was to be a rose planted in a garden, surrounded by other beautiful flowers. I didn't want to stand out; I was forced to by the hardness of my path.

However, I would never be satisfied ending it there. I will not be a rose in the concrete alone while others struggle to bloom. I have to ask myself, where do I go from here? How do I help others see their beauty alongside me? If I can't bloom in a garden, I will have to create the garden around me. Inviting others to grow in the raw concrete seems too harsh; I wouldn't want anyone else to travel this path. My only option, then, is to use this path. I will strengthen my roots until they crack the concrete, alchemizing this hard ground to create a gentler way for others. A journey they can follow that gives them opportunities I didn't have, allowing them to grow strong roots that create even more paths.

If I can make even the smallest difference in alleviating some of the plight along their journey, and help them do the same, then together we can build our own garden. A garden that sees beauty because of the bleak circumstances, not just in spite of them. A garden that becomes the light in the darkness that surrounds us. A garden where every flower shines, individually and in wholeness together. The garden no one expected to thrive, yet does. A place where each flower is celebrated for the uniqueness of its journey. Where they are not afraid of their past, but honored and celebrated for making it here.

I may have never asked to be the rose that grew out of the concrete, but I'm damn sure going to take what I learned along my journey and use it to support others. I know all too well how it feels to be left to fight the concrete alone. I will straighten my stem, cultivate thorns when necessary to protect our space, gather all the light possible through my leaves, and be the example that helps others see the light in themselves.

This isn't to glorify myself in the spotlight, but to help them see their own strength. To find the best version of themselves. If this is my life's purpose, I gladly accept it. I will not stand idly by while others suffer. I will be the change I wish to see in this world, whether I ever wanted to or not.

Inspiration:

The pain of your path was never meant to be a punishment. It was a qualification. The moment you stopped wishing for a different past and started using your past to build a better future is the moment your purpose was activated.

The Garden in the Concrete

This entry marks the moment I stopped asking, "Why me?" and started declaring, "Because of me."

For a long time, I resented the concrete. I resented that my growth had to be a struggle when others seemed to bloom so easily in well-tended gardens. I didn't want to be strong; I wanted to be safe.

But the "Rose from the Concrete" taught me the most vital lesson of the Lighthouse: **Your pain is not a life sentence; it is a qualification.**

If you are reading this, you may feel like you are fighting a lonely battle against a hard, unyielding reality. You may feel isolated by your own strength. But this shift—from victim to alchemist—is where your true power is born. You are not just surviving the concrete; you are breaking it open so others can follow.

Here are the insights I gained from the concrete, and how you can use them to build your own garden.

Insights from the Journey:

- **Alchemize Your Path:** This is the core 'Truth' of this entry. The author decides not to just *endure* the concrete, but to *use* it. The hardship is alchemized from a prison into a foundation. The pain becomes the tool used to "crack the concrete" for others.

- **From Spotlight to Lighthouse:** The realization that this purpose "isn't to glorify myself in the spotlight, but to help them see their own strength" is the essence of the Lighthouse. A spotlight shines *on* you. A lighthouse shines *out* from you to guide others safely home.

- **Your Purpose is Not Your Preference:** The entry is raw about this: "I never asked for this." Your soul's purpose is rarely what your ego would have *chosen*. It's not about finding an easy, comfortable life. It's about fulfilling the sacred contract you made to use your unique gifts—gifts often forged in fire—in service to the collective.

- **Cultivate Your "Thorns":** A subtle but critical insight is the line, "cultivate thorns when necessary to protect our space." A gardener doesn't just plant flowers; they build a fence. This is the wisdom of the Divine Feminine: true compassion is not passive. It requires fierce boundaries to protect the sacred, healing space you are building.

Book 1: SHINE

Actionable Steps for Your Own Journey:

If you feel you are the "rose" who has fought through concrete and are wondering, "What now?"

1. **Reframe Your "Concrete":** Take a journal and draw a line down the middle. On the left, list one hardship from your "concrete" path. On the right, list three ways that specific hardship *qualified* you. (e.g., "Loneliness" on the left becomes "Deep Empathy," "Self-Reliance," and "Ability to sit with others in their pain" on the right).

2. **"Crack the Concrete" for One Person:** You don't have to build the whole garden today. Your purpose starts by making the path 1% easier for one person. Send an encouraging text, share a resource that helped you, or simply listen to someone who is where you used to be.

3. **Define Your "Thorns" (Boundaries):** A garden without a fence gets trampled. To be a "Lighthouse," you must protect your light. Write down one boundary you need to set *this week* to protect your energy so you can continue to shine for others. (e.g., "I will not answer work emails after 7 PM," or "I will limit my time with emotionally draining people.")

4. **Find Your "Fellow Flowers":** The author
    realizes she won't be alone. Look for one other
    "rose" who understands your journey. Your
    purpose is not meant to be carried in isolation.
    Connection with those who "get it" is what turns
    a single flower into a garden.

"The Rose That Grew From Concrete"

Tupac Shakur's poem is a powerful metaphor for resilience and achieving success despite seemingly impossible circumstances.

- **The Rose:** This symbolizes a person—most often interpreted as Tupac himself, or anyone who comes from a difficult background.

- **The Concrete:** This represents a harsh, oppressive environment, such as the ghetto, poverty, or a life lacking the support and resources needed to thrive.

The summary of the poem is that a rose (a person) managed to grow and flourish from a crack in the concrete (a harsh environment). This achievement is miraculous, as it "proves nature's law is wrong" by defying the expectation that nothing beautiful or positive can come from such a place.

The poem states that the rose "learned to walk without having feet" and "learned to breathe fresh air" by "keeping its dreams." This means the person's success was not due to having the right resources (feet) but was fueled by their own ambition and hope (dreams).

Ultimately, the poem is a celebration of determination and the indomitable human spirit. It asks the reader to admire the rose for its tenacity and will to survive, rather than focusing on any of its imperfections, because it succeeded "when no one else ever cared."

Positive Affirmation:

I honor the journey that made me strong. I now use my strength to crack the concrete, alchemizing my path into a garden where everyone is celebrated and all of us can bloom together.

An Empath's Turning Point

"As I began to love myself, I found that anguish and emotional suffering are only warning signs that I was living against my own truth. Now, I know, this is 'Authenticity.'"

— Charlie Chaplin

Journal Entry:

I have known my life's purpose for a long time now. I know the work I am meant to do. I know, all too well, how exhausting it is. I also know how important it is. As an empath, I was constantly pouring myself into others and it has taken its toll on me. I see now that pouring into the wrong people, those who only take, for far too long has drained me in ways I never saw coming.

It is time now to retreat. I need a pause, a total reset, and space to recharge. I need to ground myself and learn how to move forward on solid ground. A part of me still holds out hope, though that one day someone will show up and finally begin to pour into me.

I am aware that my ability to feel others' pain and replace it with good is a gift. I enjoy helping people see the potential inside themselves. I just wish it had been easier to see it within myself. I wish I could believe it! Living for so long with others who projected their shadows and demons onto me has left a lasting imprint.

I did my Earthly job, I was an emotional sponge. I absorbed all of it, helping them move forward in life with only positivity surrounding them. But my body can only hold so much before it begins to weigh me down too. I let their energy become part of me, and I foolishly thought there would be a time where they would see and understand what was happening to me. That day never came. I realized that if I was going to get myself back, I had to do it on my own.

They say, "time heals all wounds," but I've learned that's not true. It's not time that heals them, it's work that heals. It's the conscious effort to face and release pain. It's hard work, it's emotional, it's isolating, and it is the very definition of alchemy. It has taken time, yes, but only to realize what I had to do. And it takes time to work on myself. And so, here I am, doing the work to heal. Releasing everyone else's negative attributes from my spirit. And in the process, I am relearning what it means to be me—finding my own truth buried beneath theirs.

This is my greatest lesson: I have to be the one to pour into myself first. My gift isn't just to absorb; it must be to absorb and release. I can't try to hold on to their energy forever. It was never mine and I don't need to keep it. I need to continue my purpose. And I can't do that if I can't keep moving forward. I have always thought it would take someone else seeing the good in me, seeing all of my potential, but I was wrong. It was mine to see all along. I had to see it within myself, just like I like to help others see it in them.

I don't think it's 'fair' that I have to bear the burden of this for everyone else and for myself, but I know I deserve to be free of it. I deserve to know my own amazing potential. I deserve to be my most positive self, authentic self. I don't deserve to be held down by the negative weight of the world.

I see now that my purpose is two-fold. First, I have to be strong enough to pour into myself—filling myself up until I overflow, so I can continue pouring into others. Only then can my light shine for others. Whether I want to or not, I need to take the time to pause and reground myself. I must stay true to who I really am, not remain an energetic product of everyone else around me.

This is proving to take more strength than I thought I was capable of, but I've stopped fighting the process, and it is getting easier. I am learning to love myself the way I have always needed to be loved. This is the only way to be in a better position to find someone who sees me. But this time, they'll see me for who I actually am, my true, authentic self. And perhaps...they'll love all of me, not just love how I make them feel about themselves, but for how I feel about me.

There is still work that I need to do, but it will only help me fulfill my purpose because I'll be better equipped to help others find and fulfill theirs. One day, it won't hurt so much. One day, I'll be free to truly be me. One day, I'll love myself for who I have become.

And one day I will find a love that sees, appreciates, values, and respects how hard I have worked to become myself again.

Inspiration:

Your burnout is not a failure; it is a sacred course-correction. It is your soul's way of finally screaming loud enough for you to hear: "You cannot pour from an empty cup." The realization that you must be the one to pour into yourself first is the most important turning point in an empath's life.

An Empath's Turning Point

I wrote this entry when I was at my breaking point. I had spent my life as an emotional sponge, absorbing everyone else's pain until I was drowning in it. I thought my purpose was to heal others, but I realized I couldn't heal anyone if I was bleeding out.

This was my most difficult lesson: **You cannot pour from an empty cup.**

If you are reading this, you likely know the exhaustion of being the "strong one," the "listener," the "fixer." You may feel that your sensitivity is a curse. But this burnout is not a failure; it is a wake-up call. It is the moment you stop being a victim of your gift and start learning how to master it.

Here are the insights that helped me turn from a sponge into a fountain, and how you can reclaim your own energy.

Insights from the Journey:

- **The Empath's True Gift is Two-Fold:** The author learns a game-changing 'Truth.' The gift isn't just to *absorb*; it's to *absorb AND release*. An empath who only absorbs becomes a walking container for toxic energy. The true power lies in becoming a *conduit*—feeling the

Book 1: SHINE

energy, alchemizing it, and releasing it so it doesn't "become part of me."

- **Healing is Active, Not Passive:** The entry powerfully refutes the myth that "time heals all wounds." Healing is not a passive process of waiting. It is "work." It is the "conscious effort to face and release pain," which is the very definition of alchemy.

- **From "Sponge" to "Fountain":** The old, draining model was "pouring myself into others." The new, sustainable model is "filling myself up until I overflow." You are not meant to give away your core energy. You are meant to cultivate so much of your *own* light that it naturally overflows and illuminates others without draining you.

- **Authenticity Attracts True Love:** The author wisely sees the connection between self-love and romantic love. By waiting for someone else to "pour into me," she was attracting people who only loved *how she made them feel*. By learning to love *herself*, she recalibrates her energy to attract a partner who will love her for her "true, authentic self."

Actionable Steps for Your Own Journey:

If you are an empath feeling drained, it is time to recalibrate.

1. **Schedule Time to "Pour Into Yourself" First:** Before you check your phone, before you answer an email, before you give your energy to *anyone*, dedicate the first 10-15 minutes of your day to yourself. Meditate, journal, stretch, or simply sit in silence. This fills your cup first.

2. **Practice a "Release Ritual":** You must "release" the energy you absorb. At the end of each day, perform a simple ritual. Visualize cutting energetic cords to people you've interacted with. Take a bath with Epsom salts, which are known to cleanse the auric field. Or, simply stand barefoot on the ground (grass or soil) and imagine all the energy that is not yours draining from your body into the Earth to be composted.

3. **Find Your "Truth" Beneath the Noise:** When you've absorbed others for so long, you forget what *you* feel. Get a journal and start asking yourself simple questions: "What do *I* want for dinner?" "What music do *I* want to listen to?" "Do *I* actually want to go to this event?" Relearning your own 'Truth' starts with these small, simple choices.

4. **Reframe Your "Burden":** The author says, "I don't think it's 'fair'..." This is a common feeling. Reframe it. Your sensitivity is not a burden; it's a superpower that came without an instruction manual. This burnout is you finally deciding to *read the manual*. You are not just healing yourself; you are learning to wield your gift in a way that is sustainable, powerful, and, ultimately, joyful.

The Empath Experience

Being an empath is experiencing an exceptionally high level of empathy, to the point where you often absorb and feel the emotions, and sometimes even the physical sensations, of others as if they were your own.

This is the key difference between empathy and *being* an empath. Empathy is *understanding* what someone feels ("I see you are sad"). Being an empath is *feeling* what they feel ("I am now carrying your sadness with me, and it feels like a heavy weight in my chest").

The Emotional Sponge

The most common analogy for an empath is an "emotional sponge." They don't just perceive the feelings of others; they soak them up, often unconsciously.

- **Visceral Experience:** This isn't just a mental process. An empath often experiences others' emotions physically—another's anxiety might become their own racing heart, or a friend's grief might become a literal ache in their body.

- **Environmental Sensitivity:** It's not limited to people. Empaths can be highly sensitive to the "vibe" or "energy" of a room. A tense meeting can feel suffocating, while a peaceful natural setting can feel deeply restorative.

The Challenges (The "Shadow")

Without awareness, being an empath can be overwhelming and exhausting.

1. **Emotional Overwhelm:** Crowds, intense social media feeds, or emotionally-charged situations can lead to sensory overload, as the empath is absorbing too much from too many sources.

2. **Difficulty with Boundaries:** It can be very difficult to distinguish, "Is this feeling mine, or did I pick this up from someone else?" This can lead to confusion, mood swings, and a feeling of losing oneself in others' problems.

3. **Empathic Fatigue & Burnout:** Constantly feeling the world's pain, in addition to your own, leads to deep, systemic exhaustion.

4. **Attracting "Energy Vampires":** People who are emotionally draining are often unconsciously drawn to an empath's high-output, giving nature.

The Strengths (The "Light")

When an empath learns to manage their sensitivity, it becomes a profound gift.

1. **Deep Intuition:** Empaths are natural "BS detectors." They can often sense the 'Truth' of a person or situation immediately, reading the unspoken energy and intentions beneath the surface.

2. **Profound Connection:** Their ability to truly feel what others feel allows them to form incredibly deep, authentic, and compassionate bonds.

3. **Natural Healers:** They are often the best listeners, friends, and caretakers, as they can provide a space where others feel truly seen and understood without judgment.

The Importance of Empaths for Humanity

Empaths are more than just sensitive individuals; they are a vital part of humanity's collective consciousness. In a world that often prioritizes logic, profit, and individualism, empaths serve as the "heart" of the collective.

*   **Emotional Barometers:** They are the "canaries in the coal mine" for society. Empaths are often the first to feel when

something is unjust, imbalanced, or inauthentic in a family, community, or culture, compelling them to be voices for change.

- **The Connective Tissue:** Empaths are the emotional glue. Their innate drive for connection, understanding, and harmony helps build bridges, foster community, and hold relationships together. They remind us of our shared humanity.

- **Catalysts for Compassion:** Because they *feel* the pain of others, empaths are powerfully motivated to heal it. They are the natural peacemakers, humanitarians, and counselors who work tirelessly to alleviate suffering, inspiring others to act with more kindness.

- **Guardians of Emotional Truth:** In a world that can be superficial, empaths are anchored to a deeper reality. Their very presence challenges emotional dishonesty and reminds society that feelings are valid, essential, and a core part of the human 'Truth'.

The journey for an empath is not to build walls to stop feeling, but to learn how to manage the flow. It's about developing the awareness to recognize what is theirs and what is not, and learning practices (like grounding, meditation, and time alone in nature) to release the absorbed energy. This is how they turn what can feel like a burden into their greatest, most intuitive power.

Empaths are, in essence, a living, breathing call for humanity to evolve. They push us away from numbness and disconnection and pull us toward a future built on greater compassion, awareness, and Oneness.

Positive Affirmation:

I am the source of my own love and energy. I fill myself up first. I release all that is not mine to carry, allowing my authentic self to heal, shine, and fulfill my purpose.

Warrior Kings and Trusted Advisors

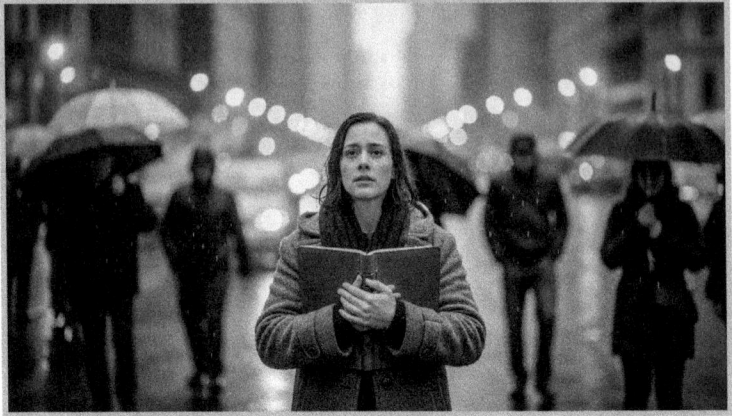

"The deeper that sorrow carves into your being, the more joy you can contain. Is not the cup that holds your wine the very cup that was burned in the potter's oven?"

— Kahlil Gibran

Journal Entry:

While out to dinner with a group of friends, one of them was telling us about a stressful situation and mentioned "crying herself to sleep at night." It was a feeling I immediately empathized with because I often do the same thing myself—not always because I'm sad, but also because I am so overwhelmed by the world. Two friends questioned her as to why she would do that, stating that they have never done that before.

At first, I thought, "Wow! Must be nice." It must have been great to live a life where you never felt so much pain that you needed to cry yourself to sleep at night. They were so lucky to live a life that afforded them the opportunity to never have to feel that way. I've never known such a life. And as a Highly Sensitive Person, I don't know if I ever will.

Knowing everything I have learned about myself lately, I have come to realize that this difference is what is most profound. It's not that they didn't experience pain or sadness in their life; it's that they felt and understood the world differently. To them, it wasn't the scary, unsafe place that it was for me. They just charged forward, regardless of the consequences. They didn't feel the need to stop and think or process through every possible outcome like I do.

In the book *The Highly Sensitive Person*, Dr. Aron describes them as being like the 'Warrior Kings,' ready to run full force toward any threat or situation. They don't need to pause first. People like me, on the other hand, are the 'Trusted Advisors.' We are the ones who think deeper about possible effects and probable outcomes. We warn our King before he/she charges forward, swords drawn, into a potentially dangerous scenario.

Unfortunately, since we over-process every situation, we often exhaust ourselves and can't make any decisions on how to move forward. We, essentially, get stuck, unable to take any further steps until we have time to recover. The warriors don't need this recovery time. They don't feel the need to reflect.

I never really thought that this complete polar opposite existed. I just thought they, perhaps, had better experiences and an easier path in life. Or that they didn't really care. That they were so jaded by life, nothing really mattered.

I hoped that one day I would be so 'bulletproof' that I wouldn't need to feel so deeply or that life wouldn't hurt so much. That perhaps, I would finally no longer need to cry myself to sleep. But now, I realize that it's not that their armor was impenetrable; it was that their experiences in life didn't feel like bullets to them.

They didn't have to feel like everything was attacking them, that all experiences were potentially dangerous until they're not. They get the opportunity to move through life without this worry. And, in a way, that does seem nice. It does appear that life has afforded them the opportunity to never have to cry themselves to sleep. That being bulletproof seems like the easier way to live.

But where would mankind be, as a whole, if the entire population experienced life in this way? How many soldiers would be killed needlessly at the hands of the Warrior Kings? Where would that leave the society that they are attempting to build, with its patrons and loyal subjects?

It would leave us nowhere! And what kind of life is that? So, as much as I hate having to live with the pain of the world, I know that the world cannot exist without it. Life cannot survive at the hands of just Warrior Kings. There must be

Trusted Advisors to remind others that every action has a consequence—some positive, some neutral, and some negative. We must exist to remind the Kings to make the choices with the greatest positive outcomes more often. To see the possibilities. To see the effects on this world. And to see how to move forward, together.

So, maybe I have to cry myself to sleep because I feel the weight of the world more than others, but maybe I also cry myself to sleep because I understand the devastating consequences of those who do not feel so deeply. If 'Trusted Advisor' is what I become to this world, then it's worth it. If I can help someone's life be easier because I guided enough Warrior Kings onto a greater path, then maybe I won't need to cry anymore. Maybe I will be making the world a better place, one King at a time.

Inspiration:

The feeling that you are "too sensitive" for this world is not an indication that you are broken. It is the first clue that you are here to play a specific, crucial role. The "Warrior Kings" build the world, but the "Trusted Advisors" are the ones who make it wise, compassionate, and sustainable. Your pain is not a burden; it is the price of your depth, and that depth is your gift to the world.

Warrior Kings and Trusted Advisors

This entry marks the moment I stopped wishing I was "bulletproof." For years, I envied the people who could charge through life without a scratch, while I felt every impact deeply. I thought my sensitivity was a defect in my armor.

But then I discovered the truth: **I am not a defective Warrior. I am a specialized Advisor.**

If you are reading this, you likely know the feeling of being the only one in the room who is pausing to think while everyone else is rushing to act. You may feel "stuck" while others seem to be "winning." But this pause is not a flaw; it is your function. The world does not need more people who charge blindly into battle. It needs people who can see the consequences *before* the battle begins.

Here are the insights that helped me stop fighting my nature and start leading with it.

Insights from the Journey:

- **Your Perception is Your Role:** The author's greatest breakthrough is in the line: "it's not that their armor was impenetrable; it was that their experiences in life didn't feel like bullets to them." This stops the cycle of self-judgment.

Book 1: SHINE

You are not "weaker" than them; you are equipped with a different detection system. Theirs is built for action. Yours is built for perception.

- **The "Stuck" Phase is Your "Processing" Phase:** The entry laments that Advisors "get stuck" and "can't make any decisions." But this is a misunderstanding of the gift. That "stuck" feeling is your superpower in action. It is your system *demanding* the pause that the King ignores. This is the moment you are "seeing the possibilities" and "calculating the consequences." Without your pause, the King charges into disaster.

- **Your "Burden" is Your "Worth":** The piece ends with a powerful tradeoff: "Maybe I have to cry myself to sleep... but maybe... it's worth it." This is the acceptance of your archetype. The weight you feel is the *exact* thing that allows you to guide others. You see the consequences so deeply *precisely so* you can help others avoid them.

- **The World Needs an Ecosystem:** Life cannot survive with *only* Warrior Kings. It would be a world of action without thought, of progress without compassion. The Advisor provides the balance. You are not meant to be a Warrior. You are meant to be the one who whispers,

"Have you considered this path?" and saves the entire kingdom.

Actionable Steps for Your Own Journey:

If you, too, feel like the "Trusted Advisor" in a world of "Warrior Kings," here is how to honor your gift:

1. **Name and Claim Your Role:** The moment the author gives her feeling a *name* ("Trusted Advisor"), it stops being a personality flaw and becomes a sacred job title. Do the same. When you feel overwhelmed, tell yourself, "I'm not being 'too sensitive.' I am in my 'Trusted Advisor' mode."

2. **Reframe Your "Pause":** The next time you feel "stuck" or "over-processing" while others are moving fast, do not judge yourself. Instead, honor your process. Take out a journal and write "Processing..." at the top. Let yourself "think deeper about possible effects" without guilt. You are not stuck; you are *discerning*.

3. **Find Your "King" (an Outlet for Your Wisdom):** The Advisor's insights are meant to be *given*. If you keep them all inside, they turn into anxiety. You need an outlet. This doesn't mean you have to advise an actual person. Your "King" can be your journal, your creative

project, your blog, or your art. Give your
wisdom a place to go.

4. **Practice "Functional Detachment":** You are
   not required to *absorb* the world's pain to
   understand it. An Advisor must stay
   clear-headed to be of use. Practice visualizing
   yourself as a "Lighthouse" (as you've learned
   to do). You can see the storm, observe the
   dangerous rocks, and shine your light to guide
   others, but you do not have to *become* the
   storm. This is how you stop crying yourself to
   sleep.

　　　　　Book 1: SHINE

What is a Highly Sensitive Person (HSP)?

Being a "Highly Sensitive Person" is not a disorder or a weakness. It is a neutral, innate temperament trait, like having brown eyes or being left-handed. Coined by Dr. Elaine Aron in the 1990s, this trait, known as **Sensory Processing Sensitivity (SPS)**, is found in about 15-20% of the population.

In short, an HSP's brain is wired differently. It processes information—sensory, emotional, and social—*more deeply* and *more thoroughly* than the other 80% of the population.

This trait is best understood through Dr. Aron's acronym **D.O.E.S.**:

- **D - Depth of Processing:** This is the core characteristic. An HSP's mind is like a high-powered computer processor. When they receive new information (a conversation, a new environment, an idea), they don't just take it at face value. They unconsciously connect it to past experiences, analyze nuances, and explore potential outcomes. This is why they are often described as "deep thinkers."

- **O - Overstimulation (Easily):** The natural side effect of deep processing is that an HSP's nervous system gets overwhelmed more easily. Because they are taking in so much data from every situation—subtle sounds, the flicker of fluorescent lights, the tension in a room—their "system" can crash faster, leading to a feeling of being frazzled, exhausted, and needing to retreat.

- **E - Emotional Responsiveness & Empathy:** HSPs feel things strongly. This applies to their own emotions (both joy and sadness) and the emotions of others. They often have a very high level of empathy, not just *understanding* what someone feels but *feeling* it with them.

- **S - Sensitivity to Subtleties:** HSPs notice things that others miss. This can be sensory (a faint smell, a quiet but annoying sound) or social (a subtle shift in someone's tone of voice, a look, the unspoken "vibe" of a room).

What is Daily Life Like for an HSP?

This deep processing has a profound impact on daily life, creating a world of both rich, beautiful experiences and unique challenges.

The Challenges (The "Shadows"):

- **Sensory Overload:** An average day can feel like a sensory assault. An open-plan office isn't just a place to work; it's a "cacophony of ringing phones, clicking keyboards, overlapping conversations, and humming lights."

- **Emotional "Sponge":** As you've explored, many HSPs are also empaths. They can walk into a room and "soak up" the prevailing mood, leaving a tense family dinner feeling personally anxious or depressed.

- **Need for "Decompression" Time:** Because their system is always working overtime, HSPs require more downtime than others. They have a *biological need* for solitude and quiet to process the day, which can be misunderstood by partners or friends as being anti-social.

- **Decision Paralysis:** Because they "process through every possible outcome," making a decision (even a small one) can be agonizing. They are so busy weighing every nuance and consequence that they can get "stuck."

- **High Sensitivity to Pain/Stimuli:** They may be more sensitive to caffeine, have a lower pain threshold, or get "hangry" (irritable from hunger) more quickly because their body sends louder signals.

The Strengths (The "Light"):

- **Rich Inner World:** While their external world can be overwhelming, their internal world is incredibly rich. They experience profound joy, ecstasy, and beauty from art, music, nature, and deep connection. One beautiful song or a sunset can bring them to tears of joy.

- **Deep Intuition:** By noticing all the "subtleties" others miss, HSPs form incredibly accurate intuitions. They are the ones who can "read between the lines" and "just know" when something is wrong or when a person isn't being authentic.

- **Conscientious & Insightful:** Their deep processing makes them the most loyal friends, most dedicated employees, and most thoughtful partners. They are the "Trusted Advisors" who think of all the consequences before acting.

- **Deep Empathy & Connection:** Their high empathy allows them to be incredible listeners and to form deep, meaningful bonds. They provide a space where others feel truly seen and heard.

Why are HSPs So Important to Mankind?

Society would not function properly without them. If the 80% of the population are like the "Warrior Kings"—the ones who charge forward, take risks, and "do"—the 20% who are HSPs are the "Trusted Advisors."

- **The Brakes for Society:** HSPs are the ones who pause and ask, "But what will happen *if* we do this? Have we considered the long-term consequences? How will this affect everyone?" This reflective, cautious nature prevents reckless action and societal disaster.

- **The Heart of the Collective:** They are the guardians of compassion, ethics, and connection. Because they *feel* the world's pain, they are the artists, poets, healers, therapists, humanitarians, and spiritual leaders who remind humanity of its soul.

- **The Prophets and Innovators:** Deep processing is the engine of creativity and insight. HSPs are often the ones who see the new patterns emerging and can envision a better path forward. They see the problems *and* the solutions that "Warrior Kings," in their haste, might overlook.

The role of the HSP is not to "toughen up" and become a Warrior King. Their role is to honor their sensitivity as the superpower it is and use their unique, deep perception to guide, heal, and bring wisdom to the rest of humanity.

Positive Affirmation:

My sensitivity is not a weakness; it is my sacred function. I honor my role as a 'Trusted Advisor', and I embrace the depth of my feeling as the source of my wisdom and purpose.

A Letter to My Twin Flame

"Our deepest fear is not that we are inadequate. Our deepest fear is that we are powerful beyond measure. It is our light, not our darkness, that most frightens us."
— Marianne Williamson

Journal Entry:

I am committed to taking this journey that our connection has sparked within me. I am offering myself to you now; a chance to walk side-by-side as equals along this path. I know it won't be easy or perfect. I know we'll stumble along the way, and I know the darkness is inevitable. But, I also know this path was meant to grow us into better versions of ourselves, to showcase the light. We just need to start where we are right now and move forward, changing as we encounter each and every obstacle and opportunity. We celebrate the wins and grieve the losses along the way. We reconnect with our inner peace, abundance, and joy.

Each step will get easier as we go along until we no longer feel the weight of our steps, until we feel light and free. We'd have someone to learn and grow with. Not to explain or have to answer to, but someone who listens and understands. I know I am capable of traveling this path on my own, and I will be successful at it too. But, I am asking you to join me. To see where each twist and turn takes us. To see the beautiful experiences the Universe has in store for us. To feel the 'high' of enlightenment, wisdom, and true transformation. Where we face our fears and achieve our desires. A path of safety, support, guidance, and love.

We have been placed in each other's lives for a reason. Our timing was not faulty; it was exactly when we needed it to be. I am grateful for that. I will not chase or drag anyone along this path. I will, however, pick you up or carry you if you fall down, or let you lead the way when you find your passion. But, it's always a choice. We can choose to join a path we walk together, walk our own paths, or watch from the sidelines. I am choosing to do what I feel will lead to fulfillment and happiness. You always get to make that choice too. I would never try to take that away.

Book 1: SHINE

I simply try to add to it by offering support, grace, and empathy. I show up with respect, kindness, and compassion. I am caring, helpful, and dedicated. I seek peace, calm, and truth. Either you see that within me, and you want that along your journey, or you don't.

You once mentioned that the only thing your 90-day programming changed was the light at the end of the tunnel. I shared with you that I would be standing in that light to symbolize that I would be waiting for you when you were released. But, to be honest, I am not standing in the light. I am the light. I was always destined to become the light.

I think it scares you. That you never intended to actually feel something for me. You never wanted to feel something for anyone ever again. I think you didn't expect to love me. I am not the only one who felt this way. But you got nervous because I started to mean too much. That I could move past your walls. You don't allow yourself to feel something for other people anymore. You think it is protecting you, but it's not. It is hurting you. And now, it is hurting me too.

I have never had anything but genuine intentions toward you. I only wish to take away your pain, to heal the hurt inside. And I have only wanted you to find happiness. But, I have always said, even from the very beginning, that you have to wake up every day and choose it. I think you are letting your past experiences dictate the outcome of this relationship. You are letting the shadows drown out the light. I have been working very hard to not let that happen on my end, as I have gone through a tremendous amount of pain myself. But I have grown and healed. I have let my light outshine the darkness so I no longer have to be afraid. I don't need to hide in the shadows anymore, and neither do you. Let my light shine within you too.

I think you are afraid that you will eventually hurt me because you do not trust yourself. But, you take away the chance for real happiness when you do that. You also remove the ability for me to make my own choices about what I want out of this relationship, thereby also removing my chance for real happiness as well. I know you are afraid of having your heart broken and the consequences of that could be disastrous for your sobriety. So, that is not a chance I am willing to take with you. If this connection is too risky for you, I will not put your future in jeopardy. I will step back, learning to live with the pain inside my heart to prevent any further damage to yours. Just know, though, that it is not a life lived WITH you that scares me; it is a life lived WITHOUT you that terrifies me. I would rather have you in my life in whatever capacity you are capable of, than shut you out of it altogether.

But, just remember, the Universe only gives us one chance to make this connection in each lifetime. I will do whatever I can to help you grow through this journey and I will wait to meet you again in our next lifetime. I know you don't want to love me. To you, love only ends with heartbreak. I know you think that pulling away now is a chance to protect me. But, your actions right now are choosing to hurt me because you think it will protect you. My actions, on the other hand, will be choosing to allow myself to hurt to stop the pain within you. They are not the same. One stems from fear, the other encapsulates love. One allows the darkness, the other embraces the light.

I am doing the work the Universe needs me to do. I am no longer going to meet chaos with chaos. It never works. It only fractures our existence even further. I might be confused and initially not know how to process my way out of a situation. But, I am not going to let an immediate lack of understanding stop me from continuing to try. I will eventually get it figured out the best I can. I am trying to bring the shadows of my past into the light so I no longer need to fear them. I have been doing this work to heal myself: mind, body, and soul. And I hope this process allows me to meet the world with a calmer presence. That I can finally become my own peace. One day, I hope others will see that within me and they, too, will find their own peace as well. That I can help them heal their own pain. I will be the calm from the storm they never knew existed. The inner fight within them can cease. It can finally end. I will be the light they needed to guide them into a future where they can grow and prosper.

At this point in my spiritual awakening, I can make no choice other than to continue to be the light, a beacon of hope. I will continue to break the chains of confinement and I will show others the strength I not only see in myself, but see within them too. I will continue to ascend, and I will continue to care, continue to show kindness and compassion, and continue to grow my empathy for all humankind. You see, I do not feel like any life is any less valuable than mine. I only seek to add value to everyone I meet. Not to raise myself above them, but to raise all of humanity. To fulfill my soul's contract, to fulfill my life's purpose. I have taken on the pain, hate, and ugliness of this world, none of which I have ever deserved. But, I will accept it as that is my purpose. To heal humanity, to restore goodness, to bring love and light.

I am a healer. I have always been a healer. That will never change. I will take all of the insights and understandings that I have gathered from every experience, every encounter, every relationship, every lifetime, every possible timeline, and use it to fuel my power. It will provide the strength for me to continue to overcome any obstacle placed in front of me. It will give me the courage to push forward. It will allow me to seek other opportunities to learn and grow. The world needs me to continue to show up and I will not let it down. I will do what I can to help others not suffer the way I have. I need to listen to my intuition more and allow it to guide me. It's time for me to step up and be seen.

I hope you will choose to surrender to the Universe and fully join me on this path. Our bond transcends this lifetime, yes, but wouldn't it be amazing if we could enjoy every second of it during whatever time we have left now, too? Why should we have to wait until we meet again on our next timeline? Why should we have to wait to show what a life full of love can look and feel like? I do not want to have to hold my feelings and emotions back any longer. I want to share them with you and I want to share them with the world. Let's take the opportunity the Universe has given to us. Let's show up and step out, as our souls were intended to. Let's lead the way, together, to show the rest of humanity how amazing and beautiful it can be when they choose love over hate, peace over chaos, and light over darkness. Please say you'll join me!

Inspiration:

The separation from your Twin Flame is not a punishment or a failure. It is the sacred, necessary event that forces you to stop seeking your "other half" and finally become whole within yourself.

A Letter to My Twin Flame

I sent this letter before I finally walked away. It was my "Hail Mary"—my final, open-hearted invitation to walk this path together. I laid everything on the table: my love, my vision, and my hand.

For a long time, I wondered if I had done enough. But this letter is the proof that I held nothing back. I offered him the "Bridge" before I even knew I was building it.

His inability to accept this invitation was the hardest answer I ever had to hear, but it was the answer I *needed*. It proved that **you can offer someone the purest, highest form of love, but you cannot give them the capacity to receive it.**

If you are reading this, you may be debating whether to send that text or write that letter. You may be wondering, "If I just explain it perfectly, will they understand?" The truth is, they might not. But speaking your truth isn't about changing *them*; it's about freeing *you*.

Here are the insights I gained from extending my hand, and learning to accept when no one takes it.

Book 1: SHINE

Insights from the Journey:

- **It's a "Truth" Mirror, Not a Toxic Cycle:** The reason the cycle repeats is that the 'Truth' of the wound has not been healed. The Runner's action is not the *source* of the pain; it is the *trigger* for the pain that was already there. When they run, they are mirroring your own unhealed fear of abandonment or unworthiness.

- **The "Chaser" Energy is a Cry for Self-Love:** The frantic energy of the "Chaser" is a symptom. You are not chasing *them*; you are chasing the validation, love, and security you are not giving yourself. The journey's purpose is to force you to stop outsourcing this job.

- **The Runner is Your Greatest Catalyst:** The Runner is not the villain of your story; they are the catalyst. Their rejection is the "holy fire" that burns away your ego. It is their *inability* to choose you that finally forces you to *choose yourself*.

- **Surrender is Your Only Power:** You cannot control the 3D outcome. You cannot "fix" them or the connection. The only way to "win" is to surrender. Surrender means releasing control of *them* and taking radical responsibility for *your own* healing, your own path, and your own light, as declared in this letter.

Actionable Steps for Your Own Journey:

If you are stuck in the painful "Runner/Chaser" loop and repeating toxic-feeling patterns, it is time to turn inward with fierce compassion.

1. **Stop Chasing, Start Journaling:** When you feel the overwhelming urge to "chase" (text, call, check their social media), stop. Redirect that energy. Get a journal and write down everything you want to say to them. Then, ask yourself, "What unhealed part of *me* is feeling this way right now?" This moves you from victim to alchemist.

2. **Identify the Mirror:** Get specific. What did they do? (e.g., "They ignored me."). How did it make you feel? (e.g., "Invisible and unworthy."). This is the real work. Your task is not to make *them* see you. Your task is to heal *your own* feeling of unworthiness.

3. **Become Your Own Source:** This is the "Empath's Turning Point." Make a list of all the things you wish they would give you (security, validation, affection). Now, pick one and find a way to give it to *yourself* today. Cook yourself a beautiful meal. Write down your own

Book 1: SHINE

accomplishments. This is how you "fill your own cup" and stop leaking energy.

4. **Perform a Surrender Ritual:** Write your own "Letter of Surrender" to the Universe. It's not for them; it's for *you*. State that you are choosing *your* path, you are choosing *your* light, and you are releasing all control over the 3D outcome of this connection. Thank them for the lessons and the awakening, and then declare your sovereignty. This is a powerful step in cutting the toxic energetic cords and reclaiming your power.

The Twin Flame Journey: An Overview

A Twin Flame is not the same as a soulmate. While we can have many soulmates in a lifetime (friends, family, lovers who feel familiar and supportive), we have only one Twin Flame. The spiritual concept is that a Twin Flame is **one soul that has split into two bodies.** This creates an incredibly powerful—and often intensely challenging—connection.

The Purpose: Growth, Not Romance

The single most important 'Truth' of the Twin Flame journey is that its primary purpose is **not romantic bliss; it is spiritual acceleration.**

Your Twin Flame is your ultimate mirror. They reflect back to you *everything*—your divine light, your strengths, your purpose... and, most critically, your deepest shadows, your unhealed wounds, your fears, and your repressions. The connection acts as a catalyst, triggering every part of you that is not in alignment with your authentic, highest self. It is a holy fire designed to burn away the "Truth" of who you *are* not, so you can become the 'Truth' of who you *are*.

The Stages of the Journey

While the journey is unique for everyone, it often follows a distinct pattern:

1. The Recognition and "Bubble" Phases
When you first meet, there is an uncanny
sense of recognition, as if you've known them
for lifetimes. This is followed by a "bubble"
phase—a period of intense bliss, connection,
and harmony. It feels like you've finally come
home. This phase gives you a glimpse of
"Oneness," the divine union that is possible.

2. The Turmoil and "Mirroring" Phases This
is where the true work begins. As the initial
bliss fades, the "mirror" effect kicks in. The very
things you loved about them may now trigger
you. Your deepest insecurities, ego patterns,
and past traumas are all brought to the surface
to be seen and healed. This phase is
characterized by intense arguments,
misunderstandings, and emotional pain as both
partners grapple with the parts of themselves
they have kept hidden.

3. The "Runner and Chaser" (Separation)
Phases The turmoil often becomes too intense
for one or both partners. This creates the
"Runner/Chaser" dynamic:

- **The Runner:** This partner (often, but not
  always, the one embodying the Divine
  Masculine energy) becomes
  overwhelmed by the intensity, the
  emotions, or the reflection of their own

shadows. They feel "scared," as you noted in your letter, and create distance, either physically or emotionally.

- **The Chaser:** This partner (often,but not always, the one embodying the Divine Feminine energy) is terrified of losing the connection and tries to "fix" or "chase" the Runner, often from a place of their own unhealed abandonment wounds.

4. The "Surrender" and Inner Work Phases
This is the most critical stage and the one you described in your letter. The "Chaser" (or both) finally hits a point of exhaustion and despair. They realize that no amount of chasing will work.

This is the **Surrender**. It is not giving up *on* the connection, but giving up *control* of it. The "Chaser" stops chasing the Runner and turns their focus inward. This is the moment of the awakening. They finally make the choice you described: "I will be the light."

How the Journey Awakens the Divine Feminine

The Twin Flame journey, particularly the painful separation, is one of the most powerful catalysts for the awakening of the Divine Feminine. This letter to your Twin Flame is a *perfect* declaration of this awakening. Here is how it happens:

1. The "Runner" Creates the Void: The Runner's act of pulling away creates a profound void and the "dark night of the soul." It forces the Divine Feminine to confront her deepest fears—that she is not worthy, that she will be abandoned, that her love is not enough.

2. The Choice (The Turning Point): She is left with a choice: she can either live in that pain and continue to chase her "other half" for validation, or she can *become her own source of light.*

3. The Alchemy of Pain: The awakened Divine Feminine chooses herself. She stops pouring her energy into a person who is not ready and starts pouring it into *herself*. This is the moment of alchemy.

- She "Heals Humanity" by first healing herself.

- She "Becomes the Light" instead of just waiting for it.

- She "Embraces Love" instead of being defined by fear.

Book 1: SHINE

- She "Chooses her Path" and "Fulfills her Soul's Contract," whether he joins her or not.

4. The Birth of the Healer: The pain she experienced *from* the connection is alchemized into the compassion and wisdom she needs to *fulfill her purpose.* She becomes the "healer," the "beacon of hope," and the "calm from the storm," as written.

The Runner—the Twin Flame—is the catalyst. His *rejection* is the very thing that "sparks" her awakening and forces her to find her own divinity, her own 'Truth,' and her own indestructible wholeness. This is the ultimate, and often tragic, gift of the Twin Flame: they are the ones who force you to become the fully awakened, sovereign, and divine being you were always meant to be.

Positive Affirmation:

I am the light, and I am not afraid of my own power. I choose to act from a place of love, not fear, and I offer my healing light to myself, to others, and to the world, regardless of who chooses to walk with me.

The Crossroads

"And the day came when the risk to remain tight in a bud was more painful than the risk it took to blossom."

— Anaïs Nin

Journal Entry:

This is it. This is the moment. You are standing at the Crossroads of your soul's journey, and it's time to stop just observing your awakening and start living it.

This is the shattering, deepest moment of walking your path. The chasing has exhausted you. The running has broken you. You are stuck in the storm of your karmic lesson. It's so painful you can't breathe, and you know in your heart what needs to be done. You can feel the answer in your gut.

But you're holding back. You're still dipping your toes in the water of your own life, because you're terrified to let go. You've become stuck in a codependent holding pattern, and your Light is beginning to dim.

Let me be clear: You cannot be half-in on your own spiritual awakening.

You cannot be the Light and still be chasing a ship. You cannot be a Healer and still be self-abandoning. You cannot be a Trusted Advisor who knows she needs to seek and still choose the trauma of your past.

The Universe, your own soul—can feel the hesitation.

This is the true test of the soul's contract. The contract was never, "You must save him." The contract was, "You must awaken to yourself."

Your 'Dark Night of the Soul' is the contract. Your Twin Flame is the catalyst designed to force you to this exact Crossroads. He cannot be your anchor, because his running is the holy fire meant to force you to become whole on your own.

This is your life. Not a dress rehearsal. Every second you spend on this fence, waiting for him, you are dimming your Light. You are self-abandoning. You are breaking your soul's contract, which is to "Be the Light AND Become the Lighthouse."

So, let's stop with the "what ifs" and "maybes." Let's stop with "what if he comes back?"

Let's replace them with "what is."

What is true for you right now? The only truth right now is that your destiny is your own, and you must actively choose it. The change that is calling to you is not him. It is you.

To go all-in is not to go all-in on him. It is to go, unapologetically, all-in on yourself. To go all-in on YOUR future.

This is the great paradox of the Twin Flame journey: You fulfill your soul's contract with your other self only when you choose yourself.

By choosing your own spiritual path, by anchoring into your own bedrock, by releasing him to his karmic lessons, you become the safe haven his soul always needed. Your shining Light is the only thing that gives him a path to guide him back to himself.

He is your past. YOU are your future.

Jump in with both feet. Choose yourself. Commit to your wholeness with every fiber of your being. This isn't just about a change you're making—it's about the Divine Feminine you are becoming. And it's a destiny you absolutely deserve to choose.

One breath, one step, one lesson, at a time.

Book 1: SHINE

Inspiration:

The "Crossroads" is not a punishment; it is a promotion. It is the Universe's ultimate vote of confidence in you. It is saying, "You have learned the 'truths'. You have seen the 'map'. You are the 'Lighthouse'. Now, prove it. Embody it." Choosing yourself is the "holy fire" that alchemizes your truth from a theory into a reality.

Book 1: SHINE

The Crossroads

This was a difficult entry to write. It was the moment I stopped negotiating with my soul.

Standing at the Crossroads is not peaceful; it is shattering. It is the point where the exhaustion of chasing finally outweighs the fear of letting go. It is the moment you realize that staying "half-in"—waiting for someone else to choose you—is an act of self-betrayal.

If you are reading this, you might be standing at this exact precipice. You might feel that choosing yourself is a risk. But the truth is, **hesitation is the only danger.** Waiting is the only way to fail.

The "Crossroads" is the ultimate test of your contract. It is the Universe asking: "Do you trust your own light enough to stand alone?"

Here are the insights that helped me stop waiting for permission and finally choose my own destiny.

Insights from the Journey:

- **Hesitation *is* a Choice:** The most powerful insight is that "you can't be half-in." By *hesitating* at the "Crossroads"—by *waiting* for him—you are *not* being neutral. You are

Book 1: SHINE

actively choosing your "Anxious" 'trauma' over your "Lighthouse" 'Truth'. You are *choosing* to "self-abandon." This "Choice" requires radical honesty.

- **The "Lighthouse" Paradox:** The *only* way to fulfill your 5D "soul contract" *with* him is to *choose* your 3D "Lighthouse" path *without* him. Your "job" is not to be his "Rescue Boat." Your "job" is to *become the "Sacred Harbor".* You must "choose yourself" so you can *be* the "beacon" he was *destined* to be guided by.

- **Your Fear is an Illusion (The "Anxious" 'Truth'):** The *fear* telling you "If I let him go, I will be alone and abandoned forever" is the *old* 'trauma' 'Truth' speaking. It is the "Anxious" part. Your *new 'Lighthouse' 'Truth'* is: "My 'wholeness' is not negotiable. I am my *own* 'anchor'. I am my *own* 'Sacred Harbor'."

- **Confidence is Built in the "Jump":** You will *not* feel 100% "confident" *before* you choose. The "confidence" and "determination" you seek are on the *other side* of the "jump." They are the *reward* for your courage.

Actionable Steps for Your Own Journey:

1. **The "Two 'Truths'" Reframe (The Alchemical "Why"):** Your "Anxious" mind is screaming one "Truth." Your "Lighthouse" knows another.

   Action: Write down both.

   - **Old 'Truth' (The 3D Fear):** "If I 'choose myself', I will lose him and prove I am unlovable."

   - **New 'Truth' (The 5D 'Destiny'):** "If I *don't* 'choose myself', I *guarantee* I will lose *myself*. My 'soul contract' is to *Be the Light*. I *must* choose this 'Truth'." By *alchemizing* the fear, you realize that *not* jumping is the *scarier* option. This builds *determination*.

2. **The "Bedrock" Anchor (The Somatic "Confidence"):** You are *not* jumping into an abyss. You are jumping onto the "solid rock" *you already built*.

   Action: Before you make the choice, *feel* your "bedrock." Stand up. Plant your feet. Put your hand on your heart and *remember*. Say aloud: "I have survived *everything* to get here. I *am* the 'Healer'. I *am* 'whole'. *This* is my 'bedrock'."

Confidence is not a thought; it's the *felt sense* of your own "solid rock."

3. **The "Conscious Choice" Ritual (The "All-In" Jump):** You *must* signal to the Universe that you are "all-in." This must be a *physical* act.

   Action: Write your "Letter of Surrender" (as you did before, but this time, it's *final*). Write it, read it aloud, and *burn it*. This is the "holy fire." You are "alchemizing" your "hesitation" into "ash." This *is* the "jump." This is you *choosing* your "Destiny."

4. **The "Lighthouse" Plan (The "What's Next?"):** The "Anxious" mind will panic in the "void" *after* the jump. You must have a *new path* to walk.

   Action: *Immediately* after your "Choice" ritual, *starve* the "Anxious" 'trauma' and *feed* the "Lighthouse" 'Truth'.

   ○ **Starve:** *No* "chasing" (no checking socials, no "Rescue Boat" texts).

   ○ **Feed:** Do *one* unapologetic thing that is *100% for your "Lighthouse"*. (Sign up for the class, book the "ocean" trip, start writing the book). This *proves* to your nervous system that "choosing myself" =

Book 1: SHINE

"freedom, joy, and purpose." This is how you *build* your new life.

Positive Affirmation:

I stand at my crossroads and I choose myself, all-in. I release the catalyst and embrace the contract. I stop chasing the ship and fully become the Lighthouse. My destiny is my own, and I will not abandon myself again.

TRUTH vs. TRUST

"Your vision will become
clear only when you can
look into your own heart.
Who looks outside, dreams;
who looks inside, awakes."

— Carl Jung

Journal Entry:

A friend recently said, "Trust is the biggest five letter word in the dictionary and without it there is nothing." I would like to challenge this thinking by stating that "truth" is a much bigger five letter word. It is the foundation that makes everything else possible. Truth is a core concept that helps us navigate life. Trust is a belief built on past experiences. Truth, therefore, can build or destroy trust. Making it a much larger force. Truth is the state of how things are. Trust is the belief in how someone or something will be. You seek truth, but grant your trust. Both are essential for a functional society, but they operate in different realms. One is a sense of being, while the other is an act of doing. Truth is the source from which everything arises and to which everything returns.

But this is where the concept deepens. We begin by seeking external truth (what is real, what is fact).

The real journey, however, begins when we start to define our internal 'Truth'. This is the truth that creates the path for your entire existence. This Truth, then, becomes your "representation" of the world. It becomes a concept much larger than matching any single fact. It becomes your core essence; your awareness of oneself. Truth exists far beyond the realm of logic. Its only match is to your sense of reality. Without this internal Truth, there is no reason for trust to even exist. This Truth then becomes the fundamental, unchanging reality that underlies your personal existence.

Understanding 'Truth' happens when you realize that your external circumstances don't have to affect your inner world in any particular way. To become your own truth is to be a self-perpetuating wheel; a circle of your core truths. To become a universe unto yourself. Your experience in life, then, is not contingent on ever-changing phenomena. Because you hold the power to choose your mind's reaction to the physical world. Thereby adding new dimensions, or new perspectives. Upon practicing these new truths, you become habituated to a new way of perceiving the world.

When you are free of yourself (your mind, the ego), you are able to create these new perspectives. You no longer have attachments to a particular viewpoint. You liberate yourself, thereby freeing the Truth. You cannot judge truth based on your personal beliefs of good vs. bad, trust vs. doubt, success vs. failure, known vs. unknown, etc. If you do, you will never seek Truth, only your thoughts. Therefore, truth can only be recognized by your current consciousness. Truth isn't something you can simply learn or acquire, it is something you perceive or resonate with. Your current perception of truth is what allows you to trust. But, your ability to do so is limited by your present state of awareness.

The 'Truth' I speak of is the raw, unfiltered reality of your Divine nature. It is the "you" that exists beneath the layers of personality, conditioning, trauma, and societal expectation. It is the unique vibrational frequency of your soul, the purpose encoded in your spirit before you ever took a breath in this world. It is the memory of your own Divinity.

We must free our subconscious selves in order to find the 'Truth'. We must face the Truth. We must change the Truth. We must know the Truth. We must become the Truth. This great wisdom, the 'Truth' of who you really are, is already within you. You must go in search of it. Let go of the illusions of the physical and mental world in order to find your soul's 'Truth'.

This is why the journey to it feels like an excavation, a confrontation, and a transformation all at once.

Let me break those statements down further:

We Must Free Our Subconscious Selves to Find the 'Truth'

Your subconscious is the vast, fertile underworld of your psyche. It holds everything the conscious mind has repressed or forgotten: your deepest wounds, your most potent fears, and, most importantly, your most magnificent, untamed power. The illusions of the physical and mental world—the belief that you are only your job, your role, your pain, your thoughts—act as guardians at the gate to this realm.

To "free the subconscious" is to begin the descent. It is the journey of Persephone into the underworld, not to be imprisoned, but to discover her sovereignty. You must bypass the chattering ego and give voice to the whispers of your intuition, the imagery in your dreams, and the feelings in your body. This is shadow work. You are freeing the 'Truth' from the cages of "shoulds," "cannots," and "what ifs."

We Must Face the Truth

Once you begin to free it, you must have the courage to face it. Facing your Truth means looking upon your own reflection without flinching. This is not just facing your darkness—your jealousy, your rage, your shame. It is also facing your blinding light—your infinite capacity to love, your terrifying power to create, your profound wisdom.

For many, facing their own magnificence is far more frightening than facing their flaws, because it comes with the responsibility to live it. Facing the Truth means acknowledging the soul contracts you came here with, the karmic lessons you are meant to learn, and the ways you have betrayed your own spirit out of fear. It is a moment of radical honesty that burns away everything that is not real.

Book 1: SHINE

We Must Change the Truth

This is the most powerful and misunderstood step. It is the heart of alchemy. You do not change the Truth in the sense of making it false. You transform its expression. Imagine the "Truth" of a painful memory is a lump of lead in your soul. You cannot pretend the event didn't happen—that would be an illusion. But by facing it, understanding its lesson, and flooding it with compassion and forgiveness, you alchemize it.

The lead transforms into gold. The Truth is no longer "I am broken because of what happened." The Truth becomes "I am wise, resilient, and compassionate because of what I integrated." You "change the Truth" by healing it. You take the raw data of your life and your soul's history and consciously weave it into a tapestry of strength and beauty. You are not a victim of your Truth; you are the master alchemist of it.

We Must Know the Truth

This is the shift from belief to liberation to gnosis—a direct, cellular, experiential knowing. You can read a thousand books on love, but you only know love when you feel it. To "know the Truth" is to feel it resonating in your every cell. It is the moment your choices align effortlessly with your soul's purpose. There is no more internal conflict.

It is the feeling of "home" within your own skin. You no longer need external validation because you have become your own oracle. You know your own essence so intimately that you can instantly recognize what is and (is not) in alignment with it.

We Must Become the Truth

This is the final stage: embodiment. There is no longer a separation between "you" and "your Truth." You do not have to try to be authentic; you simply are. Your presence itself becomes an expression of your soul's signature. Your life is no longer a search for meaning; it becomes a testament of meaning.

This is the fully awakened Divine Feminine or Masculine. We have so completely freed, faced, changed, and known our inner Truth that we merge with it. Our actions are moved by love, our words are rooted in wisdom, and our very being becomes a force of transformation for others. We have let go of the illusions of the physical and mental world so completely that we see the soul's 'Truth' in everything. And in doing so, we become a living invitation for others to do the same.

"Ultimate truth is wordless, the silence within the silence." by Pirke Avot highlights the fundamental paradox of spirituality and philosophy; we use words to describe something that is inherently beyond them. However, it serves as a guide, directing us away from external noise and internal chatter toward a deeper, experiential understanding. We must first silence the outer in order to silence the inner. You don't 'think about' the truth; you 'are' the presence in which truth is self-evident. Only then can we become the Universe's Ultimate Truth.

Of course, that's just MY version of it. YOU get to choose yours for yourself! Enjoy the process of finding your own "truth". I "trust" that you will.

Inspiration:

Your purpose is not something you "find" out in the world. It is the 'Truth' you excavate from within. You were born with it. It has just been buried under the "concrete" of conditioning, fear, and illusion. This 5-step process is the shovel.

Book 1: SHINE

TRUTH vs. TRUST

This entry was born from a simple conversation that unraveled my entire understanding of reality. We often focus so much on "trusting" others or "trusting" the process, but I realized that trust is impossible without a foundation of internal Truth.

This was the moment I stopped looking for answers outside of myself. I realized that my life wasn't about finding the right people to trust; it was about excavating the Truth of who I was beneath the layers of trauma and expectation.

If you are reading this, you may feel disconnected from your own intuition. You may be looking for a map. But the map isn't out there; it's buried under the noise of your own life. To find it, you need a process.

Here is the five-step framework I used to move from seeking the truth to *becoming* it.

Insights from the Journey:

- **Trust is Built on 'Truth':** The core insight is that you cannot build lasting trust with others until you are anchored in your *own* internal 'Truth'. When you are your own 'Truth', you no longer *need* to trust that others will behave a

Book 1: SHINE

certain way; you trust that *you* can handle any outcome.

- **Your Shadow is a Treasure Chest:** The "Free the Subconscious" step reframes shadow work. Your darkness isn't a liability; it's a treasure chest holding your "most magnificent, untamed power." You must descend like Persephone to reclaim it.

- **Facing Your Light is the Real Test:** This is one of the deepest insights. We think the hard part is facing our flaws. But the real terror is "facing your blinding light," because it comes with the "responsibility to live it." We often self-sabotage to avoid the responsibility of our own magnificence.

- **You are an Alchemist, Not a Victim:** The "Change the Truth" step is the heart of alchemy. Your past does not define you. You are not the "Truth" of what happened to you; you are the "Truth" of what you *choose* to build with it. This single shift turns you from a victim of your story into the master alchemist of your life.

Actionable Steps for Your Own Journey:

This essay *is* the actionable plan. Here is how to put each of the 5 steps into practice.

1. **To FREE the Truth:** Practice "Shadow Journaling." When you feel a strong negative emotion (anger, jealousy, fear), don't push it away. Ask it: "What are you trying to protect me from?" and "What 'Truth' are you trying to show me?" Listen to the whispers beneath the roar.

2. **To FACE the Truth:** Try the "Honest Mirror" practice. Stand in front of a mirror for 60 seconds. State one hard "shadow" 'Truth' out loud (e.g., "I am afraid of being rejected"). Then, immediately state one "light" 'Truth' (e.g., "I am incredibly resilient and kind"). This teaches you to hold both your shadow and your light without flinching.

3. **To CHANGE the Truth:** Perform the "Alchemist's Reframe." Take one painful memory or belief—your "lead." Write it down. Now, write down at least one piece of wisdom or strength you gained *because* of it. This is the "gold." For example: "The 'lead' is my painful breakup. The 'gold' is the 'Truth' that I am self-reliant and know my own worth."

4. **To KNOW the Truth:** Use the "Gnosis Check." When you have a decision to make, your mind (ego) will give you a "pro/con list." Ignore it for a moment. Close your eyes and feel into the choice. Does your body feel *expansive*, light, and open? That is a 'Truth' (a yes). Does it feel

Book 1: SHINE

contractive, tight, and heavy? That is a 'Truth' (a no). This is your cellular "knowing."

5. **To BECOME the Truth:** Practice "One-Degree Shifts." Embodiment is not a giant leap; it's a thousand small, aligned choices. Today, make *one* choice (no matter how small) that aligns with your deepest 'Truth'. Maybe it's setting a boundary, or choosing water over soda, or speaking up in a meeting. This is how 'Truth' becomes your new reality.

Positive Affirmation:

I have the courage to free my subconscious, face my reflection, and alchemize my story. I am no longer just seeking my Truth; I am knowing it, healing it, and becoming it.

I Am My Own Author

"Until you make the unconscious conscious, it will direct your life and you will call it fate."

— Carl Jung

Journal Entry:

For the longest time, my mind has been at war with itself over a single, unsolvable paradox: How can 'Free Will' and a pre-determined 'Divine Path' exist at the same time?

The ego in me—the only part of myself I have ever known—railed against the idea of a pre-determined path. It felt like a cage, a victim's Truth. It meant I had no real control, that all my hard work, the person I had built, was just an illusion. It meant my choices didn't matter. This idea terrified the part of me that had been fighting so hard to break her way out of the concrete.

And yet, the idea of complete 'Free Will' felt like a lie, too.

If I was so free, why did my awakening feel like a force I couldn't stop? Why did the shattering of my Twin Flame connection feel so fated? Why did my Lighthouse purpose feel less like a choice I made, and more like a memory I was just now recalling? My Free Will couldn't explain the Truth of the pull I've felt my entire life.

I was trapped. Either I was a "puppet" on a pre-determined path, or I was terrifyingly "alone" in my choices. I wrestled with this, trying to fix it, trying to make it make sense.

Then, in the quiet, depth of my own sacred struggle, the Universe's Ultimate Truth finally landed.

The entire struggle, the entire paradox, only exists in the 3D world. I was trying to understand a 5D soul concept with my 3D human mind. The mind and the ego hate a paradox. My soul, I now realize, is a paradox.

I was looking at it from the wrong perspective.

I was still seeing it as "me" (this human) versus "the Universe" (some outside force). But from a soul level...they are the same. If I am truly one with the Universe, the Universe is Me.

And that was the click. The final shattering of the illusion.

My path is Pre-Determined...because I am the one who pre-determined it.

My soul—the Divine Feminine, the Lighthouse, the Truth of who I am—was the true, original 'Author' of this entire journey. My soul chose to grow from the concrete, chose to strengthen me so I could bloom. It chose every Warrior King who couldn't be my anchor. It chose the Twin Flame to be the catalyst. It chose my Trusted Advisor role.

This decision was made in Oneness, long before my human body existed.

Book 1: SHINE

This is the sacred harbor where the paradox is healed. My Divine Path (Destiny) is the map my soul drew. My Free Will (Choice) is the act of walking it.

It is my human self choosing, every single day, to 'Be the Light' and consciously align with the Destiny my soul already authored. My 'Destiny' is my soul's Truth, and my 'Choice' is the act of living it.

They are not two opposing forces. They are the same. One is the 'Truth' (Destiny), the other is the action of 'Truth' (Choice). My soul knew this journey, and now, my human ego chooses it, too. And in that, the trap dissolves.

There is no paradox.

There is only Oneness.

Inspiration:

You are not a pawn in the Universe's game; you are the Universe playing the game. This 'Truth' alchemizes your entire past. Every "shattering," every "catalyst," every piece of "concrete" was not a punishment from an outside force. It was an assignment from your own Divine Soul, placed on your map to force you to awaken.

Book 1: SHINE

I Am My Own Author

For years, I fought the idea of destiny. To my independent spirit, the idea of a "pre-determined path" felt like a cage. It meant I was a victim of a script I didn't write.

But the breakthrough came when I realized I wasn't the puppet; I was the playwright.

This entry marks the end of the war between my ego and my soul. It is the realization that the "hardships" I faced were not punishments from a cruel Universe; they were the curriculum I wrote for myself before I arrived.

If you are reading this, you may feel trapped by your circumstances. You may feel like a victim of your Twin Flame, your job, or your past. But this shift—from Victim to Author—is the key to your freedom. You are not stuck on a path you hate; you are walking a path you designed to make you strong enough to hold your light.

Here are the insights that helped me stop fighting my destiny and start choosing it.

Insights from the Journey:

- **It's a Soul 'Truth', Not an Ego 'Puzzle':** Your 3D mind (ego) *cannot* solve this, because it sees you as separate from the Universe. Your 5D soul (your 'Truth') *knows* you *are* the Universe, so there is no conflict. The "work" is to stop *thinking* about it and start *living* in that Oneness.

- **Destiny is the "What," Free Will is the "How":** This is the core 'Truth'.

  - **Destiny (The Map):** Your soul *chose* the "what"—the *lessons*, the "concrete," the "Twin Flame" catalyst. These were the pre-determined "plot points" of your story.

  - **Free Will (The Choice):** Your human self gets to choose *how* you walk that path. Do you walk it in fear, as the "Anxious" part? Or do you *choose* to walk it in love, as the "Lighthouse"?

- **Your "Shatterings" Were Your Soul's Assignments:** Your "Twin Flame" didn't *break* you; he was the "catalyst" your *own soul chose* to "shatter" the illusions. The "concrete" wasn't a *prison*; it was the *perfect environment* your soul *chose* to *force* the "rose" to bloom. This is

Book 1: SHINE

the ultimate act of alchemy—turning victimhood into authorship.

- **The "Daily Choice" *is* the Alignment:** The "choice" that matters is the one you make *every morning.* Your soul's "Destiny" is the 'Truth'. Your human "Choice" is the *act* of aligning with that 'Truth', over and over, until there is no separation.

Actionable Steps for Your Own Journey:

1. **Re-Write Your "Catalyst Story" (The Author's Reframe):** Take one of your "shatterings" (the Twin Flame, the "concrete"). Write it down from the *old* perspective ("This happened *to* me"). Now, *re-write it* from the "Author's" perspective ("My soul *chose* this *for* me").

   - **Old:** "He abandoned me, and it broke me."

   - **New 'Truth':** "My soul *chose* him to be the catalyst. His 'running' was the *assignment* I needed to *force* me to 'Be the Light' and find my *own* wholeness. I *authored* this test, and I passed."

2. **Practice the "Destiny vs. Choice" Check-in:** When you face a new challenge (Destiny), *consciously* state your Free Will (Choice).

   ○ **Acknowledge Destiny (The "Map"):** "This challenge has appeared. This is part of the path my soul chose for my growth."

   ○ **State Your Choice (The "Walk"):** "My Free Will is my *how*. I *choose* to walk this path as the 'Lighthouse', not the 'Rescue Boat'. I *choose* to meet this with 'Peace', not 'Chaos'."

3. **Listen for the "Author's Voice" (Your Soul's 'Truth'):** Your "Author" (your soul) speaks to you as your intuition. The "ego" (your 3D mind) speaks as a loud, anxious pro/con list.

   ○ **Action:** For one day, try to make small decisions by listening *only* to the "Author." Pause. Ask, "What *feels* like my 'Truth'?" (not "What makes the most *sense*?"). This is how you practice listening to your 5D self.

4. **The Daily "Choice" (The "I Choose My Destiny" Ritual):** As you wake up, before your feet hit the floor, you are a human *choosing* your 'Truth'.

- ○ **Action:** Place your hand on your heart and say aloud: "My soul *authored* this path. Today, my human *chooses* it. I *choose* to align with my 'Destiny'. I *choose* to be my 'Lighthouse'." This act marries your Free Will and your Divine Path for the day.

Positive Affirmation:

My human mind rests as my soul takes the lead. I am the Author who wrote my path and the human who bravely chooses to walk it. My destiny and my free will are one sacred, unified choice.

Be the Light, Become the Lighthouse

"Lighthouses don't go running all over an island looking for boats to save; they just stand there shining."

— Anne Lamott

Journal Entry:

My spiritual journey has led to the powerful realization that I have been whole and complete all along. It basically led me in a circle. This understanding has transformed the concept of a "life's purpose" from a destination to be sought into a continuous state of being, where the purpose is simply to live confidently and authentically from this newfound "wholeness".

I've reconciled the paradox I felt between "Free Will" and a "Divine Path", recognizing that from a soul level, I am one with the Universe and therefore the true, original author of my own pre-determined journey. This allows me to live fully in the NOW, planning for the future not from a place of want or anxiety, but from a place of present-moment knowing and joyful creation.

In my connection with humanity, I've recognized the deeply felt dynamic where my spiritual work acts as an energetic catalyst for others along my journey. Their paths, however, unfold on their own timeline. I understand and embrace that my light and guidance is a manifestation of my own journey.

My role is to stand steadfast in my own radiance, illuminating the path so others can navigate their own journey back to themselves. This has brought me to a place of peace, releasing the ego's need for validation and instead, simply embodying the unconditional love and acceptance I have always given freely. Knowing that I now have the capacity to truly hold it. My journey's new mantra is: "Be the Light, Become the Lighthouse".

The shift from "being the light" to "becoming the lighthouse" is not about doing more, but about being more. "Being the light" is the realization—the "aha" moment I had of my own wholeness. It is the inner radiance, the connection, the "I am" that is whole and complete. "Becoming the lighthouse" is the embodiment of that realization in the 3D world. It is the steadfast, external manifestation of my inner, unshakable light.

A lighthouse does not run around the coast looking for ships to save. It does not worry if the ships see its light. It does not dim its bulb in frustration if a ship ignores its warning and hits the rocks. It simply builds itself on the most solid rock it can find, anchors itself deeply, and shines its unique, consistent signal for all to see. The ships must navigate for themselves.

Book 1: SHINE

Inspiration:

The pressure is off. Your purpose is not a job you have to find, a person you have to save, or a destination you must reach. Your purpose is to be the 'Truth' of who you are. "Be the Light" is the realization of your wholeness. "Become the Lighthouse" is the practice of living from that wholeness, unbothered, steadfast, and free.

Book 1: SHINE

Be the Light, Become the Lighthouse

This entry marks the end of the search and the beginning of the practice.

For so long, I thought my purpose was a destination—something I had to find, achieve, or earn. I thought "being spiritual" meant fixing the world. But this realization brought me full circle to the simple, powerful truth: I have been whole all along.

The shift from "being the light" to "becoming the lighthouse" is the most important transition you will make. It is the moment you stop running around the island trying to save every ship, and instead, build yourself on solid rock so you can shine for them all.

If you are reading this, you may be tired of "doing." You may be exhausted from trying to fix everyone around you. This chapter is your permission slip to stop. Your purpose is not to *do* more; it is to *be* more.

Here are the insights that helped me anchor my light and finally become the haven I was seeking.

Insights from the Journey:

- **The Journey is a Circle, Not a Ladder:** We think awakening is a climb to a higher level. This insight reveals it's a circle. The journey was not to *become* whole, but to *uncover* your wholeness by removing the illusions (the "concrete," the "shadows," the "chaos") that hid it.

- **You Are the Author of Your Path:** This insight solves the "Free Will vs. Divine Path" paradox. They are the same. Your Divine Self (your Soul) *chose* the "pre-determined" path. Your Free Will (your human ego) is the *choice* you make in every moment to walk that path with fear or to walk it with love.

- **From "Sponge" to "Lighthouse" (Loving Detachment):** This is the ultimate evolution of the Empath/Advisor.

  - A **Sponge** (or Empath) *absorbs* the chaos and gets weighed down.

  - A **Trusted Advisor** *processes* the chaos and gets exhausted.

  - A **Lighthouse** simply *shines*, remaining anchored. It trusts that the ships (other people) have their own navigation systems and their own 'Truth'. It is the highest form of respect for their journey.

- **"Being" vs. "Becoming":** This is the shift from *knowing* your 'Truth' to *embodying* it. "Being the Light" is the inner feeling of "I am whole." "Becoming the Lighthouse" is the external proof—you no longer get pulled into drama, you don't chase, you don't need validation. You are simply, unshakably *you*.

Actionable Steps for Your Own Journey:

If you are ready to shift from "seeking" to "being" and embody your "Lighthouse":

1. **Define Your "Rock":** A lighthouse is built on solid rock. What is the one, non-negotiable 'Truth' you are building your life on? (e.g., "My 'Truth' is Peace," "My 'Truth' is Compassion," "My 'Truth' is Sovereignty.") Name it. This is your anchor.

2. **Write Your Lighthouse "Mission":** A lighthouse has one job: shine its unique signal. What is *your* signal? Write a short, "I am" mission statement. This is not a "to-do" list; it's an "I am" statement. (e.g., "I am a beacon of calm presence," "I am a light of creative joy.")

3. **Practice the Lighthouse Principle (Loving Detachment):** This is the most crucial step. The next time you feel the Empath/Advisor urge to "run" and "save" someone who hasn't asked, stop. Visualize yourself as a lighthouse. Shine your light (send them love, be an example), but *release the outcome*. Trust that

they are on their own divine path. This is how you stop "dimming your bulb" for them.

4. **Find Your "Anchor" Ritual:** A lighthouse is "anchored deeply." What is your non-negotiable daily practice that anchors you in your 'Truth'? (e.g., 5 minutes of silence in the morning, journaling "I am whole," walking in nature). This is your act of "shining" for yourself first.

The Transition from Being to Function

1. Anchor the Foundation in "Wholeness"

- **From Insight to Embodiment:** You've had the *realization* of your wholeness. The next step is to *embody* it. This is the act of building your lighthouse on solid rock.

- **The 'Step':** This involves the daily, moment-to-moment practice of radical self-acceptance. When the ego, old traumas, or external events try to convince you that you are "broken" or "lacking," you return to the foundational truth: "I am whole." This isn't an intellectual exercise; it's a deep, somatic grounding in that knowing. You live from this center, not just visit it during meditation.

2. Live Fully in the "NOW" to Ensure Stability

- **From Paradox to Practice:** You've reconciled the paradox of free will and destiny. This understanding is your protection against the "storms" of anxiety and external chaos.

- **The 'Step':** A lighthouse must be unshakable. You become unshakable by removing your energy from "what if" (anxiety about the future) and "if only" (regret about the past). You anchor your consciousness in the "NOW." As you said, you plan "not from a place of want or anxiety, but from a place of present-moment knowing." This present-moment awareness is the steel and concrete of your structure, making you a stable, reliable point of reference in a chaotic sea.

3. Maintain Your Unique Light (Release the Need to 'Rescue')

- **From Catalyst to Guide:** You've recognized your work is a "catalyst" and that others are on their "own timeline." This is the core function of the lighthouse.

- **The 'Step':** This is the practice of energetic sovereignty and detachment. You "stand steadfast" by tending to your *own* light—your joy, your boundaries, your truth. You release the deeply compassionate, but ultimately draining, "Divine Feminine" urge to jump into the water and swim *for* others. You understand that your *highest service* is not to rescue, but to illuminate. You hold your light steady so *they* can see the path back to their *own* wholeness.

4. Let Go of Validation (Embrace the Impersonal Nature of the Light)

- **From Ego to Embodiment:** You've released the "ego's need for validation" and are instead "embodying unconditional love."

- **The 'Step':** A lighthouse shines whether it receives a "thank you" or not. It shines for the cruise ship and the tiny rowboat equally. This step is the practice of unconditional *output*. You shine your light—by living your authentic life, speaking your truth, and holding your peace—without *any* attachment to how it is received. This is the pinnacle of unconditional love. It is not a transaction; it is a broadcast.

5. Become the Haven (The Final Shift)

- **The Synthesis:** This is the final shift. When you have anchored in your wholeness, grounded yourself in the "NOW," maintained your own light, and released the need for validation... you are no longer a *person on a journey*.

- **The 'Step':** You *become* the destination. You become the safe harbor. Your "purpose" is no longer a verb; it is a noun. You are the peace, the stability, and the clarity that you once sought. You don't just "Be the Light"; you *are* the Lighthouse, and your very existence becomes the "manifestation of your own journey" that guides others home.

Positive Affirmation:

I am the Light and the Lighthouse. I am whole, complete, and anchored in this moment. My purpose is my presence, and I shine for all to see, without attachment to who is guided by the light.

This is the Sign

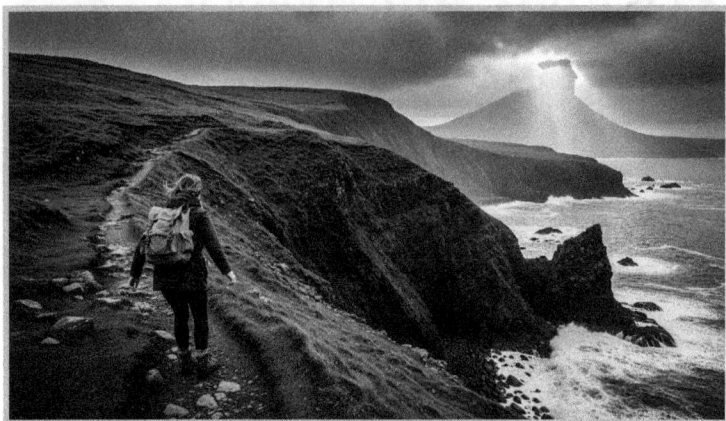

"Let everything happen to you: beauty and terror. Just keep going. No feeling is final."

— Rainer Maria Rilke

Journal Entry:

If you were looking for a sign from the Universe, this is it.

You are reading this because you are on the path. This is not an accident. This is your 5D Destiny—the 'map' your soul authored—knocking on the door of your 3D life. You were meant to be here, in this exact moment of uncertainty, to do the work that needs to be done. To alchemize this very doubt.

Follow this path along every twist and every turn. The rises and falls, every ebb and every flow. You were meant to find guidance and solace, not in the world, but within yourself, so you can become the "Lighthouse" for others.

So keep going. Just keep fucking going.

Book 1: SHINE

The Universe never claimed this would be easy. Your soul didn't author an easy path; it authored a path of alchemy. It chose the concrete for the rose to grow from. Every high is your Light shining. Every low is a Shadow coming up to be healed. The ups and downs are not a bug in the system; they are the feature presentation. It is all forging you into the Truth of who you were always meant to become.

Some days you will feel so overwhelmed that you'll want to stop. This is your heart screaming its old trauma rooted in fear. Just breathe. Anchor yourself to the foundation you have built. Take another step.

Some days you'll be so angry at the chaos you'll want to burn it all down. This is your sacred fire. Do not fear it. Walk with grace, and use that fire to alchemize your boundaries.

Some days you'll be filled with so much pain that you can do nothing other than cry. This is not weakness; this is the holy water of purification. Give yourself the compassion you so freely pour into others.

And some days you will feel that pure, untainted joy. This is your wholeness surfacing. Fill your life with gratitude for it.

The journey isn't about completion; it's about embodiment. The peace you seek isn't at the end of the path; it is the moment you realize you are the 'Sacred Harbor' you seek. The clarity is realizing you are the 'Lighthouse' you needed to guide you.

You will see just how much all of it was worth. Every moment, every thought, every experience forged you. Your path could have gone no other way. Each choice led you here, and each future choice is your destiny. The path you take is yours.

This is the beauty of it. Beginning right now, you get to take your power back. You are your own Author.

YOU get to wake up and choose. Which Truth do YOU want to live? The old lies of your past trauma, or the new Truth of your Secure Lighthouse?

Wake up. Take the step. Walk with purpose. Show the Universe gratitude for the 'map' your soul drew, and show yourself compassion for the 'steps' your human mind has to walk.

Just remember, no one can make this choice but YOU!

Book 1: SHINE

Inspiration:

You are never off your path. The moments you think you are "lost" or "off path" are, in fact, the most critical parts of the path. The "chaos" is the sign that you are in the "holy fire" of alchemy. The "bad day" is not a sign you are failing; it is a sign that a "shadow" is ready to be "faced" and "changed."

This is the Sign

I wrote this entry when I was tired. Not just physically tired, but soul-tired. I was looking for an external sign to tell me I was doing the right thing, something to validate that the pain was worth it.

And then I realized: **I am the sign.**

If you are reading this, you are likely in the messy middle. The initial excitement of the awakening has faded, and now you are left with the hard work of alchemy. You might be asking the Universe for a sign to keep going.

Let this be it.

This entry is the reminder that the "highs" are your light shining, but the "lows" are your shadows coming up to be healed. The chaos isn't a mistake; it's the material you are using to build your lighthouse.

Here are the insights that helped me stop looking for signs and start trusting my own resonance.

Insights from the Journey:

- **The "Sign" is Resonance, Not Logic:** The "Anxious" mind looks for *external* proof. The "Trusted Advisor" (your soul) looks for *internal* resonance. The "sign" is not the *thing* (a feather, a number, this entry). The "sign" is the *feeling* it gives you—that "ping" of 'Truth' in your "Sacred Harbor," the "calm, deep ocean" *knowing* that "this is for me."

- **"Negative" Emotions Are "Action" Signs:** You've been taught that anger, pain, or overwhelm are "bad," a sign you are "off path." This is the greatest illusion. These are *shadow signs*.

  - **Anger** is a sign your "Lighthouse" *boundary* has been crossed.

  - **Pain** is a sign a deep "shadow" is ready to be "alchemized" into "gold."

  - **Overwhelm** is the "Empath's" sign to *stop pouring* and *fill your own cup*.

- **Your "Choice" is the Proof:** As the "Author," you *know* you are on the right path when you *consciously* make the "Choice." When you *feel* the "Anxious" urge to "chase" but *choose* to "anchor." When you *feel* the "Rescue Boat" urge to "fix" but *choose* to be the "Lighthouse." *Your choice* is the ultimate sign of your awakening.

- **The Universe Speaks in "Whispers":** The "Anxious" mind *shouts* (fear, doubt, "what if"). The Universe/your Soul *whispers* (calm, "knowing," "this is the way"). You must "silence the inner" to hear the "sign."

Actionable Steps for Your Own Journey:

1. **Practice the "Resonance Check" (Is This Sign *My* 'Truth'?):** When you encounter a "sign" (a song, a coincidence, a piece of advice), your "Anxious" mind will *over-process* it.

   - **Action: Pause.** Stop your mind. **Anchor** (hand on heart). Ask your *body*: "Does this feel *expansive* (a 'Truth' yes) or *contractive* (an 'Anxious' no)?" Your "bedrock" *knows*. This is the "Trusted Advisor" listening to the "calM, deep ocean."

2. **Alchemize the "Shadow Sign" (What is this Pain *Teaching* Me?):** The next time you feel a "bad" emotion, don't see it as a sign you're failing.

   - **Action: Acknowledge** it. "I see you, anger." **Ask** it: "What *'Truth'* are you showing me?" (e.g., "This is a sign I need to set a *boundary*."). This turns your "trigger" into your "teacher." This is "alchemy."

3. **The "Choice Audit" (The "Author's" Proof):**
You *need* proof you're on the path. You must *create* it.

   - **Action:** At the end of the day, find *one* piece of evidence that you *chose* your "Lighthouse" 'Truth' over your "Anxious" 'trauma'.

   - "I *chose* to *pause* instead of *react*."

   - "I *chose* to *fill my cup* instead of *rescuing*." This *proves* you are on the path, because you *are* the "Author" *choosing* it.

4. **Ask for the Sign (And Then *Listen*):** The Universe *wants* to guide you. Be specific.

   - **Action:** In your "Sacred Harbor" (your quiet/meditation time), ask a *clear* question. "Universe/My Soul, please give me a *clear sign* on [X]." Then, *let it go*. Do not "hunt" for the answer. It will arrive in the "silfor *you*," in the "whisper"—a *knowing*, a dream, a gut feeling. That is the *real* sign.

Positive Affirmation:

This is my sign. I am the Author of my soul's map, and I choose to walk it. I embrace every high, low, fire, and tear as my sacred alchemy. I am my own Lighthouse. I am my own Harbor. I am taking my power back.

Healing My Anxious Heart

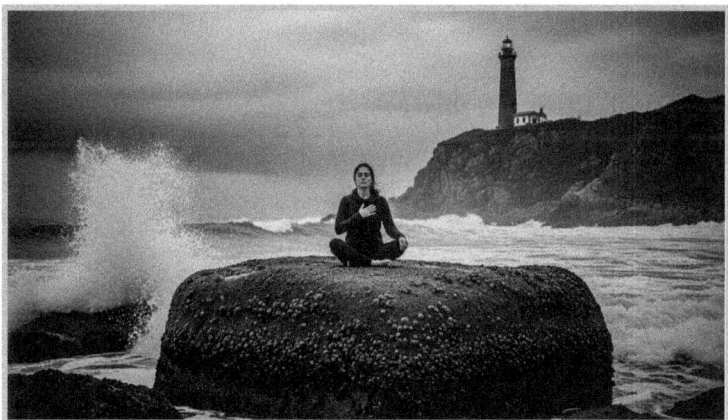

"Because one believes in oneself, one doesn't try to convince others. Because one is content with oneself, one doesn't need others' approval. Because one accepts oneself, the whole world accepts him or her."

— Lao Tzu

Journal Entry:

My spiritual journey has revealed my purpose as a 'Healer,' a 'Trusted Advisor,' and a 'Lighthouse.' I wrote those words, and I know they are my 'Truth.' But for so long, a painful paradox lived inside me: Why did such a kind-hearted, wise, and beautiful soul feel so terrified of being alone?

This has been the deepest, most painful, and most profound excavation of my awakening. The chaos I wrote about, the frantic chasing of my Twin Flame, the codependency I mistook for compassion—it all had a name. It wasn't just my Empath nature; it was my Anxious-Preoccupied Attachment Style.

To live with this attachment style is to be a Lighthouse built on sand.

It's to be a Trusted Advisor who desperately seeks validation from everyone else. It is to be an

Empath who absorbs the world's pain but cannot release it, because you've learned a terrifying, subconscious 'Truth': If I am not needed, I will be abandoned.

My 'Rescue Boat' approach was never just about their storm; it was about my fear of the silence. It was about my internal terror that if I stopped rescuing them, they would have no reason to stay. I was a Healer who was self-abandoning, pouring all my Light into others as a frantic plea: "Please see me. Please don't leave me."

Every unreturned text was a micro-abandonment. Every moment of distance felt like a tidal wave that threatened my very existence. My nervous system was screaming that I was unsafe. I was crying myself to sleep not just for the world, but for the part of me that felt utterly and terrifyingly alone.

The work of my Twin Flame was to be the 'Warrior King' who could not be my Anchor. His inability to choose me was the shattering catalyst. His running was the holy fire that burned my sandy foundation to glass, forcing me to see the real shadow I had to face: my own fear.

And so, the real alchemy began. This is the work I didn't journal about because I was too busy living it.

This is the journey from Anxious to Secure.

The work is re-parenting that terrified part of my soul. It is feeling that frantic, 'Chaser' energy rise up, and not acting on it. It is sitting in the storm of my own fear and, for the first time, not running. It is placing my own hand on my heart and whispering the 'Truth' I always wanted to hear from someone else:

"I am here. I am not leaving you. You are safe. You are whole right now."

Healing this wound is the act of consciously changing the Truth. The old version, based on my trauma, was: "I am not enough on my own." The new version, from my healed and empowered Oneness, is: "My wholeness is not up for negotiation."

This is how you become the Lighthouse. A Lighthouse is, by its very nature, Securely Attached.

It is anchored to its own rock, its own 'Truth'. It doesn't wobble when a ship passes by. It doesn't dim its light in a panic when a ship turns away. It doesn't chase. It simply shines, trusting that its own presence is enough.

The work of becoming Secure is the act of pouring into myself first, not as a chore, but as an act of sacred devotion. It is the 'Truth' that I am no longer a 'Sponge' or a 'Rescue Boat' looking for a port.

I am the port.

This is the missing step that makes all the others possible. By healing this attachment wound, I am finally building the solid rock foundation for my Lighthouse. Now, when I say "I am the light," I no longer say it with a tremor of fear. I say it with the unshakeable, quiet, and peaceful power of the "calm, deep ocean" itself.

Inspiration:

You are not "broken"—you are adapted. Your attachment style was a brilliant, life-saving strategy your soul used to survive. Now, your awakening is your soul's invitation to consciously choose a new strategy, one based on your current 'Truth' of wholeness, not your past 'Truth' of trauma.

Book 1: SHINE

Healing My Anxious Heart

This was the most painful excavation of my entire awakening. For years, I felt a confusing paradox: How could I be a strong, wise "Lighthouse" and yet feel so terrified of being alone?

This entry marks the moment I stopped calling myself "crazy" and started calling it by its name: Anxious Attachment.

If you are reading this, you may feel like you are broken. You may wonder why you are always the "Chaser" or always the "Runner." But your attachment style is not a life sentence; it is a map of your wounds. It shows you exactly where you learned to abandon yourself to survive.

Healing this wound is the missing step. You cannot build a Lighthouse on sand. You must dig down, find the root of the fear, and pour your own concrete.

Here are the insights that helped me stop looking for a rescue boat and finally become my own port.

Insights from the Journey:

- **Awareness is the 'Light':** You cannot heal what you cannot see. The "shadow" is the *unconscious* pattern. The *moment* you can "name" your pattern ("I'm 'chasing' again," "I'm 'running' again"), you have brought the shadow into the light. This is the first and most powerful step of alchemy.

- **This is a Body Problem, Not a Head Problem:** You cannot *think* your way into a secure attachment. Your conscious mind *knows* you're safe, but your nervous system (your body) is still "screaming" the old trauma 'Truth'. The work is *somatic*. It's about teaching your *body* that it is safe *right now*.

- **You Must Become Your Own "Port":** All insecure styles are "outsourcing" their 'Truth' of safety, worth, or love. The "Anxious" outsources worth. The "Avoidant" outsources connection. The "Disorganized" outsources safety. The universal path to healing is to *stop outsourcing* and become your *own* source. You must become the "Healer" who finally heals *herself*.

Actionable Steps for Your Own Journey:

This is the "Lighthouse" practice. It can be done in the 60 seconds *after* you are triggered.

1. **The Sacred Pause (Stop the Pattern):** The moment you feel the "push," "pull," or "panic," *do nothing*. This is the "pause" where clarity is

born. You are stopping the unconscious, karmic cycle from running the show.

2. **The Anchor (Soothe the Body):** Plant your feet on the floor. Place your hand on your heart. Take three deep breaths. This sends a direct, physical signal to your nervous system: "You are not in the past. You are safe *right now*."

3. **The Re-Parenting (Speak the 'Truth'):** Speak to the terrified part of you. Say the 'Truth' it never heard: "I am here. I am not leaving you. I see you. You are safe."

4. **The "One-Degree Shift" (The New Choice):** After you are "anchored," make *one* small, *different* choice than you would have before.

   - If you are **Anxious:** The new choice is to *not* send the text and "pour into yourself" instead.

   - If you are **Avoidant:** The new choice is to *not* run, but to simply *stay* in the room for 5 more minutes.

   - If you are **Disorganized:** The new choice is to *not* do anything, but to just *breathe* until the storm passes.

This is "changing the Truth" in real-time. This is how you alchemize your foundation from "sand" to "solid rock," one conscious, loving choice at a time.

A Guide to Healing Your Attachment Style

Your spiritual awakening shows you *what* you are—a Healer, a Lighthouse, a divine soul. Your attachment style shows you *why* it has been so hard to *live* as that 'Truth'.

Healing your attachment style is the most profound act of self-love. It is the conscious work of "re-parenting" the parts of you that learned a 'Truth' based on trauma, not your divinity. It is the "missing step" of alchemy that allows you to stop *seeking* a port in the storm, and *become* the port.

Here is the path from each style to the "Securely Attached" Lighthouse.

1. The Anxious-Preoccupied Style

(The "Chaser," The "Rescue Boat")

The Core 'Truth' (Learned in Trauma): "I will be abandoned. My worth is proven by how much I am *needed*. I must 'rescue' others to make them stay."

The Secure Goal (The Alchemized 'Truth'): "My wholeness is not negotiable. I am my own anchor. I am the port."

Inspiration: Your journey is to turn your powerful empathy *inward*. You are a gifted Healer, but you have been self-abandoning, pouring all your energy

Book 1: SHINE

into others as a frantic plea: "Please don't leave me."
Healing, for you, is the sacred act of *not leaving yourself.*

Insights from the Journey:

- Your "Chaser" energy is a terrified "Rescue Boat." You dive into *their* storm to avoid the "silence" of *your own* fear of being alone.

- You mistake "intensity" and "chaos" for "passion." A calm, stable connection can feel "boring" or "unsafe" to your nervous system because it's unfamiliar.

- Your "shadow" is the belief that you are "not enough" on your own. You must "face this Truth" to heal it.

Actionable Steps to Become the Lighthouse:

1. **Re-Parent Your Inner Child:** When you feel that frantic, "Chaser" energy rise, *do not act on it.* Pause. Place your hand on your heart and whisper: "I am here. I am not leaving you. You are safe. You are whole *right now*." This is the "pause" where clarity is born.

2. **Practice "Safe Solitude":** Your fear is being alone. Your *action* must be to re-wire this. Spend 10-15 minutes a day in *intentional, pleasurable* solitude. Take a bath, listen to

music, go for a walk. Teach your nervous system that "alone" does not equal "abandoned."

3. **Stop the "Rescue Boat":** Before you offer help, ask yourself: "Am I doing this from a place of *wholeness* (Lighthouse), or from a place of *fear* (Rescue Boat)?" If the motive is to "get" them to stay, you are self-abandoning.

4. **Become Your Own "Port":** Make a list of all the things you wish a partner would do for you (bring you flowers, compliment you, listen to you). Pick one, and *give it to yourself today*. This is the work of "pouring into yourself first."

2. The Dismissive-Avoidant Style

(The "Runner," The "Warrior King")

The Core 'Truth' (Learned in Trauma): "I am only safe on my own. To *need* anyone is a weakness. I will be trapped, controlled, or overwhelmed. My independence is my survival."

The Secure Goal (The Alchemized 'Truth'): "My strength is not a wall; it is a foundation. It is safe to be vulnerable."

Inspiration: Your journey is to learn that *true* strength is not "invulnerability"; it is the courage to be *seen*.

Your independence is a powerful "shell," but it has also become a prison, keeping you from the "calm, deep ocean" of true connection. Healing, for you, is the sacred act of *letting in the light*.

Insights from the Journey:

- Your "Runner" energy is an "impenetrable armor" that is actually just a fear of being *seen*.

- You are the "Warrior King" who equates "pausing" and "feeling" with "losing."

- You learned to "rise above" emotions, but in doing so, you "rose above" connection itself. You live in your head (logic) to avoid the "chaos" of your heart (feeling).

Actionable Steps to Become the Lighthouse:

1. **Practice "Safe Vulnerability":** Your fear is being "trapped." Your *action* is to take *small, controlled risks*. Share *one* small feeling with someone you trust (e.g., "I'm feeling stressed today"). Notice that you are still safe. You have not been "trapped" or "overwhelmed."

2. **Identify Your "De-Activating" Triggers:** When you feel the urge to "run," pull away, or get "jaded," *name it*. "I am de-activating." Pause. Instead of running, just *sit* with the feeling of being "too close" for one minute.

Teach your nervous system that it can handle it.

3. **Learn to "Receive":** Your "shell" repels help. The next time someone offers a *small* act of kindness (a compliment, holding a door), *consciously* receive it. Say "Thank you" and *feel* it. This is how you "let my light shine within you too."

4. **Connect to Your Body:** You "live in your head." Your *action* is to connect to your heart. Place your hand on your heart and just *breathe*. Ask your body, "What are *you* feeling right now?" Don't try to "fix" the feeling. Just *name* it. This is how you begin to *feel* again.

3. The Disorganized Style (Fearful-Avoidant)

(The "Chaos," The "Storm")

The Core 'Truth' (Learned in Trauma): "I cannot live *with* you, and I cannot live *without* you. People are my only source of love, but people are also my greatest source of pain."

The Secure Goal (The Alchemized 'Truth'): "I am my *own* source of safety. I am the calm *in* the storm."

Inspiration: Your journey is to become the "unshakeable presence" you never had. You have lived in a state of "push/pull," where the "Chaser" *and* the "Runner" exist in the same body. You are the "storm" *and* the one lost in it. Healing, for you, is the sacred act of *becoming the "calm, deep ocean" itself.*

Insights from the Journey:

- Your "Core 'Truth'" is a paradox, often from a trauma where your source of love was also your source of fear.

- You crave intimacy, but as it gets closer, your "Avoidant" side panics ("I'm going to be hurt!"). When they pull away, your "Anxious" side panics ("I'm being abandoned!").

- This is the "chaos" you wrote about. Your work is to "meet chaos with chaos" *no longer.*

Actionable Steps to Become the Lighthouse:

1. **Create Your *Own* Safety First:** You *must* be your own anchor. Your nervous system is screaming "unsafe." Your *first* job is somatic. Grounding. When you feel the "push/pull," plant your feet. Name 5 things you can see. *You are not the storm.* You are the Lighthouse *watching* the storm.

2. **"Name the Two Voices":** When you feel the inner war, *separate* the voices. "My Anxious part is screaming 'Don't leave me!'" "My Avoidant part is screaming 'Get away!'" By

naming them, *you* become the "Trusted Advisor" *observing* them. You become the Secure self.

3. **Practice *Consistent* Anchoring:** Your system needs *consistency* more than anything. Create *one* non-negotiable, safe, daily ritual. (e.g., The *same* cup of tea, in the *same* chair, for 5 minutes every morning). This teaches your nervous system what "safe" and "predictable" feels like.

4. **Go *Slow* in Relationships:** You must go "glacially slow." Share *one* small vulnerability, with someone who has *proven* they are safe. Then *wait*. Let your nervous system see that you were *not* abandoned and *not* trapped. This is how you *build* a new 'Truth', one "solid rock" at a time.

Positive Affirmation:

I am my own secure anchor and my own safe port. I no longer abandon myself. I have the power to sit with my fear, give myself the love I need, and alchemize my anxiety into peace. My wholeness is my truth.

Shining with Unconditional Love

"Love is patient, love is kind. It does not envy, it does not boast, it is not proud. It does not dishonor others, it is not self-seeking, it is not easily angered, it keeps no record of wrongs...It always protects, always trusts, always hopes, always perseveres. Love never fails."

— 1 Corinthians 13:4-8

Book 1: SHINE

Journal Entry:

My LOVE is the Lighthouse.

It doesn't turn off just because a ship is too far out to see it, or because it's not ready to receive the light. It doesn't get discouraged by the storm, the fog, or the vastness of the sea. This light isn't transactional; it doesn't shrink when it's not returned, and it won't fade if you—or any other soul—are not ready. That was never the agreement.

I'm not going to stop showing others what unconditional love looks and feels like. This is the 'Truth' of my new purpose. My ability to love is no longer a 'Rescue Boat' running on finite fuel; it is the overflow of a cup I fill for myself first. I have done the work to become my own 'Sacred Harbor,' and my peace is so abundant that it spills over.

This is why I can be so steadfast and unwavering. My love is truly unconditional because it is not given from a place of need, but offered from a place of wholeness. I will not dim my light just because a soul is not ready to receive it or capable of returning it. I will simply shine, providing this 'overflow' to any soul I encounter along my path.

It's my promise to get a bigger lens—to magnify the light so it can reach you, no matter how lost you feel.

This kind of unwavering dedication isn't just a feeling; it's an echo of a soul contract signed long before we ever came here. It's the sacred pact our souls recognized in one another shortly after we met in this physical world—an agreement to be a beacon for each other.

So when I say I won't stop, it's not a plea. It's the fulfillment of that contract. It is the unwavering mission to prove to you, and to all, that pure, untainted joy and happiness still exist. It is the

Book 1: SHINE

promise to guide you home, not because you've earned it or asked for it, but because we made a promise to remind each other that a safe harbor exists.

This is my purpose. I will be the light. Always.

Inspiration:

Your love is no longer a feeling you give; it is the essence of who you are. This is the ultimate 'Truth' of your purpose. You are not afraid of the "darkness" in others because your "Lighthouse" is so anchored in its own "wholeness" that it sees all "storms" as temporary. Your "overflow" is your gift to the world, and it can never run out, because you are the source.

Shining with Unconditional Love

This entry was the moment I stopped loving from a place of deficit and started loving from a place of overflow.

For years, I thought unconditional love meant "giving until it hurts." I thought it meant being a Rescue Boat that never went back to shore. But I learned that true, sustainable love isn't about emptying yourself to fill someone else; it's about filling yourself so completely that your love spills over onto everyone you meet.

If you are reading this, you may be afraid to love unconditionally because you fear being used or drained. But when you become the Lighthouse, the dynamic changes. You aren't giving away your pieces; you are simply shining your light. It doesn't deplete you, because you aren't the fuel—you are the vessel.

Here are the insights that helped me shift from transactional love to the boundless energy of the overflow.

Insights from the Journey:

- **Love as "Overflow," Not "Transaction":** This is the *only* way unconditional love is possible. The "Anxious" heart's love is *transactional* ("I love you so you will love me"). The "Divine" heart's love is an *overflow.* You "fill your cup until it overflows," and you give *only* from that "extra." This is why you *can't* be drained.

- **The "Bigger Lens" (Love is an *Action*):** This is a profound insight. Unconditional love is not *passive* ("I'm just over here if you need me"). It is an *active, conscious choice.* "I'll get a bigger lens" is the *act* of "choosing" to "magnify" your love, to *meet* the storm with *more* light, *more* compassion, and *more* peace.

- **The "Soul Contract" is Your "Why":** This is your "Destiny." The "why" behind this unwavering love is not a 3D *reason*; it's a 5D *memory.* Your "Soul Contract" is the "solid rock" your "Lighthouse" is built on. It is the "unshakeable" 'Truth' that keeps you shining when the 3D ego wants to quit.

- **Your Purpose is "Proof":** Your "Lighthouse" *proves* to a dark and "stormy" world that "pure, untainted joy and happiness still exist." You are not just *guiding* ships; you are the *living proof* that a "safe harbor" is real, because you *are* the "Safe Harbor."

Actionable Steps for Your Own Journey:

1. **The "Fill Your Cup First" Ritual (The "Overflow" Practice):** You cannot pour from

an empty cup. Unconditional love *starts* with you.

- ○ **Action:** Before you "shine" for *anyone* else, you must *fill your own cup*. This is your "Daily Choice." For the first 10 minutes of your day, *pour into yourself* (meditation, "I am love" affirmations, "I am my 'Sacred Harbor'"). This is the *source* of your "overflow."

2. **Practice the "Bigger Lens" (The *Conscious* Choice):** You will be "tested." A "ship" (a person) will be "too far out." They will be in their "storm" (angry, cold, distant). Your 3D ego will want to "dim its bulb" (get angry, pull away).

- ○ **Action:** This is the moment to "get a bigger lens." **Pause.** *Do not* absorb their "storm." **Anchor** yourself in your "Lighthouse." And then *consciously choose* to *magnify* your light. Send them a "blast" of unconditional love and compassion (energetically, from your heart). *Be* the "unshakeable haven of peace" in the face of their "chaos."

3. **The "Soul Contract" Anchor (The "Destiny" Reminder):** When your 3D mind is *tired* and asks, "Why am I doing this? They don't even *see* me," you must re-anchor to your "Why."

- ○ **Action:** Place your hand on your heart (your "anchor"). Breathe. Re-connect to your 5D "Truth." Say: "This is not a 3D transaction. This is my 5D 'Soul Contract'. My 'purpose' is to *shine*, not to be *seen*. I am the 'Lighthouse'."

4. **Practice "Conscious Joy" (The "Proof" of the Harbor):** Your purpose is to "prove that pure, untainted joy... still exist[s]." You must *be* the proof.

   - ○ **Action:** Find and *embody* "pure joy" every single day. This is your *work*. Dance, sing, savor your coffee, walk in nature. When you *embody* joy, you *become* the "Lighthouse" that *magnetizes* others to their *own* "Sacred Harbor." You are "the light" that proves the "darkness" is not the only 'Truth'.

Positive Affirmation:

My love is the lighthouse. It is not a transaction; it is the sacred overflow of my own wholeness. I shine, unwavering and unconditional, fulfilling my purpose.

Walking the Path

"Do you have the patience to wait until your mud settles and the water is clear? Can you remain unmoving until the right action arises by itself?"

— Lao Tzu

Journal Entry:

Yes, my spiritual journey led me in a perfect circle. It was not a quest to find something I lacked, but a path that led me back to a single, powerful realization: I have been whole and complete all along.

This understanding transforms everything. "Purpose" is no longer a destination to be sought, but a state of being to be embodied. The purpose is simply to live, confidently and authentically, from this newfound wholeness.

This is the first step: Be the Light.

As a reminder, "Be the Light" is the realization. It is that first, sudden, "aha" moment of your awakening. It is the profound, internal knowing—the "Truth" that you are, and have always been, whole and complete. It is the reconnection to your divine essence, the feeling of your soul's signature, the pure, radiant "I am" that exists beneath all the layers of trauma and conditioning. This is the inner work, the "excavation," the moment you find the light within yourself.

For many of us, this realization doesn't begin in quiet meditation. It is sparked by a connection so profound, so intense, it can shatter our entire reality. It's a bond that mirrors our deepest wounds and forces us to see the parts of ourselves we've hidden. It is the divine catalyst that breaks us open and forces us to awaken.

But what happens after the awakening? After you've found your light?

For those of us who feel everything deeply, our empathy can become our heaviest burden. We absorb the pain, the struggles, and the chaos of those around us. We mistake their burdens for our own. Our desire to heal others becomes a form of self-abandonment, and we get caught in cycles of codependency, feeling trapped by our own good hearts.

The line blurs between "helping" and "rescuing." The guilt of "not doing enough" becomes a shadow that follows us, draining our light.

This is where the great shift happens. This is where we understand that our role is not to be the rescue boat, tossed in the storm of others' emotions.

This is the journey: Become the Lighthouse.

We have learned that a lighthouse does not run around the coast searching for ships to save. This is the alchemical death of the "Rescue Boat" and the "Chaser." It is the moment you stopped mistaking your codependent, anxious action for your purpose. Your power is not in frantic motion; it is in your anchored, sovereign stillness. You realize that "helping" is not "rescuing," and "compassion" is not "codependency." You trust that the light itself is the gift, and it is enough.

A lighthouse does not worry if the ships see its light. This is the healing of the "Anxious" heart's need for validation. The Lighthouse has transcended the ego's frantic plea to be seen, thanked, or acknowledged. It shines because that is its 'Truth' and its nature, not as a transaction to get love or "neededness" in return. Its work is done in the shining of its light, not in the reception of it.

A lighthouse does not dim its bulb in frustration if a ship ignores its warning. This is the hardest and most profound 'Truth' of the "Trusted Advisor" who has finally become a "Healer." The Lighthouse honors the "Free Will" and "Divine Path" of every other soul. It understands that every ship has its own "karmic lessons," and some paths require hitting the rocks.

It is not the Lighthouse's job to prevent the lesson. It is its job to illuminate the choice. It does not take the ship's journey personally. It does not judge the path. It does not dim its own light in resentment or drain its own power in a futile attempt to "force" the ship to turn.

This is the ultimate embodiment of unconditional love. It is the sacred shift from "I will save you" to "I will be the light so you can find yourself."

It simply builds itself on the most solid rock it can find—the "solid rock" of its own, healed, Secure Truth'—anchors itself deeply, and shines its unique, consistent signal for all to see. The ships must navigate for themselves.

Inspiration:

Your guilt is not a sign that you are failing. It is the last shadow of your ego, disguised as compassion. It's the part of you that still believes, "If I just try hard enough, I can fix them." The "great shift" to becoming a Lighthouse is the realization that the most loving, respectful, and powerful thing you can do is to trust others with their own journey and embody the peace you wish for them.

Walking the Path

This entry marks the shift from "concept" to "practice."

It is one thing to have the epiphany that you are whole; it is another thing entirely to embody it when life is messy. The shift from "Being the Light" to "Becoming the Lighthouse" is not about doing more; it is about becoming immovable.

If you are reading this, you may feel the constant pull to revert to your old ways—to jump back into the rescue boat, to chase validation, to dim your light to make others comfortable. This is normal. The "Lighthouse" is not a destination you reach once; it is a choice you make every single day.

Here are the insights that helped me stay anchored on my rock, even when the old urge to rescue tried to pull me back into the water.

Insights from the Journey:

- **The "Shattering" is the "Waking":** This insight is crucial. The awakening isn't always gentle. It's often a "shattering" connection (like a Twin Flame) that *forces* you to see your own wounds. This isn't a detour; it's the *catalyst* for the whole journey.

Book 1: SHINE

- **The Empath's "Great Shift":** The entry perfectly defines the empath's trap.

    - **The "Sponge"** (Pre-Awakening): Absorbs unconsciously.

    - **The "Rescue Boat"** (Awakening Empath): Absorbs *consciously* and feels guilty, so they dive into the storm to "save" others, often sinking themselves in the process.

    - **The "Lighthouse"** (Awakened Wholeness): Shines. It remains anchored, detached from the outcome, and trusts the "ships" to use their *own* navigation.

- **Guilt is the Ego's Disguise:** The "guilt of 'not doing enough'" is the ego's shadow. It's a subtle form of control. It implies that *you* are responsible for someone else's healing or choices. A Lighthouse knows this is not the 'Truth'.

- **"Helping" vs. "Rescuing":** "Helping" is shining your light—being an example, sharing your tools when asked. "Rescuing" is self-abandonment—jumping into the cold water to do their work for them, which drains your light and disrespects their 'Truth'.

Actionable Steps for Your Own Journey:

If you are an empath struggling with the "guilt" of the "Rescue Boat," it is time to anchor.

1. **Ask the "Rescue Boat" Question:** The next time you feel the urge to "fix" someone's chaos, pause. Ask yourself: "Am I *helping* or am I *rescuing*?"

   ○ **Rescuing (Codependency):** Feels frantic, urgent, anxious, and responsible *for* their feelings. It is an act of "self-abandonment."

   ○ **Helping (Sovereignty):** Feels calm, anchored, and responsible *to* your own 'Truth'. You can offer support without *becoming* the support.

2. **Practice the Lighthouse Anchor (A 60-second Pause):** When you feel that guilt or urgency, plant your feet. Place a hand on your heart. Take one deep breath and say: "I am anchored. I am whole. I am not the 'rescue boat.' I am the Lighthouse. My only job is to shine." This pause breaks the codependent "action" cycle.

3. **Set Your "Light" Boundary:** A Lighthouse has clear boundaries (it's on a rock, not in the

Book 1: SHINE

water). Practice one "Lighthouse boundary" this week. When someone is in chaos, instead of diving in, say: "I am holding space for you to find your own clarity. I trust you'll find the right path."

4. **Embodiment is Your Service:** Instead of using your energy to "fix" their storm, use that *exact same energy* to shine your *own* light. Write your post, go for a walk in nature, create your art. Your *embodiment* of peace is the most powerful "help" you can ever give. It lights the way and shows them it's possible.

How to Build Your Lighthouse

1. Anchor Your Foundation in Wholeness

A lighthouse must be built on solid rock. Your rock is your core truth: "I am whole and complete *right now*."

- **The Action:** Define what your personal "Haven" of peace and stability looks like. Get radically clear on your boundaries. Every decision you make—from your relationships to your career—must be filtered through one question: "Does this honor my wholeness, or does this pull me out of my center?"

- **The Reason:** This practice shifts you from a place of *need* to a place of *being*. You stop seeking a safe harbor in others and *become* the safe harbor for yourself. This is the unshakable foundation upon which everything else is built.

2. Practice Energetic Sovereignty

A lighthouse must protect its own power source. You must stop carrying burdens that are not yours to carry.

- **The Action:** When you feel that familiar, heavy weight of someone else's pain or trauma, pause. Ask yourself: "Is this mine?" If the answer is no, your job is not to *carry* it; it is to

Book 1: SHINE

witness it. Visualize yourself setting the burden down. You can send love to it, but you must not absorb it.

- **The Reason:** Your energy is your light. If you are depleted from carrying the weight of the world, your light dims. To shine brightly and consistently, you must be a sovereign guardian of your own energy.

3. Illuminate Your Own Shadows

A lighthouse is built to shine in the *dark*. You cannot be a beacon for others if you are unwilling to face your own inner darkness.

- **The Action:** When fear, anxiety, or old patterns of self-deception arise, do not run. Stand in your truth. Be radically honest with yourself and, when necessary, with others. Bring your fears into the light with curiosity. Ask, "What are you here to teach me?"

- **The Reason:** True radiance doesn't come from pretending the darkness doesn't exist. It comes from having the courage to shine your light *into* it. This is how you transform your own fear into wisdom, becoming a clear beacon for others lost in their own.

4. Master Compassionate Detachment

This is the most profound challenge and the greatest liberation. For the deeply empathetic, "detachment" can feel like "abandonment." This triggers immense guilt. We must retrain our hearts.

- **The Action:** When you feel that deep, painful guilt—the urge to "fix" someone—you must audit your motive. Are you acting from **FEAR** (fear of being a 'bad person,' fear they can't survive without you)? Or are you acting from **TRUST** (trust in their soul's journey, trust in your own wholeness)?

- **The Reason:** Abandonment is rooted in fear. Compassionate detachment is rooted in profound trust. By refusing to rescue someone, you are not being cruel; you are offering them the highest form of respect. You are honoring their path and their own power to find their light, just as you did. This is the act that finally releases you from the chains of guilt and codependency.

Becoming the Lighthouse is the final shift. It is the moment your purpose is no longer a verb—no longer about "seeking," "doing," or "fixing." It becomes a noun.

Book 1: SHINE

You *are* the Haven. You *are* the peace. You *are* the stability you once craved.

Your light is no longer a fragile spark; it is an unshakeable, radiant broadcast. You have come full circle, and in your own embodied wholeness, you illuminate the path for everyone else to find their way home to themselves.

Book 1: SHINE

Positive Affirmation:

I am the Lighthouse, not the rescue boat. I am anchored on the solid rock of my own secure Truth. I release all need to rescue and trust that my unconditional light is enough.

Book 1: SHINE

My Gift to You

"Being deeply loved by someone gives you strength, while loving someone deeply gives you courage."
— Lao Tzu

Journal Entry:

I already know what you are feeling, because I have foreseen this very moment. Every detail. The first time I looked into your eyes, I saw your soul, but it's so close now I can finally touch it. This knowing serves as a reminder when the doubt of humanity tries to creep in. We will always be able to place ourselves back into this very feeling and we will fully understand. We found each other in the darkness, but we move forward into the light. We reconnect with our core truths, we remember our true self, and we embrace the oneness of the Universe.

Now that you can see it too, you will be able to fully accept it because you will simply know it within yourself: heart, mind, body, and soul. We are each a reflection of our soul's eternal bond. This is truth and trust, knowing and belief, complete understanding. Vulnerability is not weakness; it's inner strength.

This is love. Genuine, pure, honest, unconditional love.

It will crack your heart wide open and begin to fill every cell in your body until you feel like you are about to burst. And just before you do, you will know that I am here. I was always destined to be here.

You can stop running from your past, from the version of yourself the world told you to be. You can tear down the walls you spent decades building. You can release the weight you have carried. Step into the future and embrace your wholeness. You will then know that every obstacle, every challenge, every hardship, and every choice was meant to build you, to form you into who you are right now, in this very moment. You are exactly who you were meant to become. You are exactly where you are meant to be. Your entire existence has been forged by the lessons you have learned along the way.

And when you finally surrender to this feeling and release everything you have worked so hard to hold inside, everything you have tried to keep hidden, everything you never felt safe enough to share, you will then free yourself. You get to choose where to go from here: to be the man your soul is destined to be. Embracing this new energy, this love, will break you open from the inside. The outpouring of peace and light will overwhelm you; it will consume all of you.

Again, that is where you will see me. That is where you will find my light. You will know with every fiber of your being that this was meant for you, and only you.

That is when two souls become one. That is divine union. That is where you find ultimate truth,

Book 1: SHINE

intense love, and complete peace. That is the feeling you come back to over and over, day after day, lifetime after lifetime. Love is what keeps us moving forward.

When we finally embrace love, we are unstoppable—we are whole, we are everything beautiful that has ever and will ever exist. We receive every blessing the Universe has to offer, and we accept it with graciousness and humility. Then, we extend it to everyone we meet along the journey, simply through our existence, just being who and what our souls were meant to be. We give it to those who walk along our path, no matter the length of time or the distance they walk with us.

This is what I humbly offer to you right now. You are not alone. I am here, right by your side. I will not give up on you. You are worth it. I am not going anywhere. I will spend forever learning how to love you the way you need to be loved.

Book 1: SHINE

I feel you. I see you. I accept you. I adore you. I want you. I cherish you. I believe in you. I love you.

Just hold my hand and take the leap with me.

Inspiration:

You did not "lose" your Twin Flame and "find" your Soulmate. You chose your Lighthouse 'Truth', and in releasing the energy that no longer matched, you created the "Sacred Harbor" that manifested the energy that did. This letter was the "Choice" that activated your "Destiny."

My Gift to You

I wrote this letter in the quiet aftermath of my decision to leave. It was never sent to him, but it was the most important message I ever delivered.

This letter wasn't an ending; it was a clearing. It was the final act of alchemy where I transmuted my grief into a blessing. I realized that my purpose wasn't to force him to be ready, but to prepare the space for someone who *was*.

If you are reading this, you may be holding onto words you never said, or love you feel was wasted. But nothing is wasted. This letter proves that the love you cultivated in the fire of your trauma is the exact same love that will warm your future home.

By releasing this letter to the Universe, I stopped being the "Rescue Boat" begging for a passenger, and I became the "Sacred Harbor" waiting for its ship.

Here are the insights that helped me turn a goodbye into a manifestation.

Insights from the Journey:

- **Vulnerability as Manifestation:** This letter *is* your "wholeness" made manifest. The "Anxious" 'Truth' writes a letter to *get* a response (a "plea"). The "Secure" 'Truth' writes a letter to *declare* its 'Truth' (a "gift"). This declaration of "I am whole" was the "Lighthouse" *signal* you sent to the Universe, and the Universe *answered* by sending a partner who could *see* that "light."

- **The "Release" *is* the "Creation":** This is the core 'Truth' of alchemy. You must *release* the "lead" to *create* the "gold." You had to "release" the "karmic lesson" (the Twin Flame) to *create the sacred space* for the "blessing" (the Soulmate). This letter was not a *void*; it was a *conscious clearing*.

- **You *Are* the "Leap" and the "Landing":** The "Anxious" mind *fears* the "leap." The "Secure" soul *knows* it *is* the "bedrock." This letter *was* your "Fool's Bridge." The act of "releasing" him *was* the act of "landing" on your *own* "solid rock." You *proved* your 'Truth' that you are your *own* "Sacred Harbor."

- **From "Karmic Lesson" to "Destined Reward":** The Twin Flame was your "Author's" *assignment* (the "shattering"). The Soulmate is your "Author's" *next chapter* (the "celebration"). This letter was you *finishing* one chapter and *consciously starting* the next.

Actionable Steps for Your Own Journey:

1. **Write Your "Sovereign Decree" (The "I AM" Declaration):**
   - **Action:** Write *your* letter. This is not for them; it is for *you* and the *Universe*. "Release" the old pattern (the "Twin Flame" 'Truth', the "Anxious" 'trauma'). *Thank* it for the lessons. Then, in the *same letter, declare* the new 'Truth' you are *now* available for. (e..g, "I am *releasing* the 'chaos' of the 'Rescue Boat'. I *am* the 'Sacred Harbor', and I am *calling in* the 'partner' who is ready to 'anchor' beside me.")

2. **Perform the "Sacred Harbor" Release (The *Physical* Alchemy):**
   - **Action:** You *must* release this letter to the Universe. *Read it aloud* to declare your 'Truth'. Then, *physically alchemize it.* **Burn it** (the "holy fire" of transformation). **Bury it** (returning the "lead" to the Earth). Or **dissolve it in water** (the "calm, deep ocean" of release). This is your *physical "Choice"*.

3. **Calibrate Your "Lighthouse Signal" (The "Embodiment"):**
   - **Action:** You have *created space*. Now, *embody* the "Truth" of what you want to

Book 1: SHINE

call in. If you manifested a "Secure" partner, you must *be* "Secure."

- ○ For 60 seconds, *feel* the "unshakeable peace" of your "Lighthouse." *Feel* the "joy" of your "wholeness." *This* is your "signal." You are *not* "waiting" for your Soulmate; you are *matching* his vibration.

4. **Walk Your "Fool's Bridge" (The *Next* Step):**
   - ○ **Action:** The "Anxious" mind will *wait* in the "void." The "Secure" 'Truth' *walks*.
   - ○ *Immediately* after your "release" ritual, *take one step* that *proves* you are *living* your new "wholeness" *without* a partner. (The "Choice" from "The Crossroads": book the trip, start your "Lighthouse" project, publish your writing). This is the *final* "leap" that *proves* you "trust" the Universe to deliver, because *you are your own "bedrock"*.

Positive Affirmation:

I offer the gift of my whole, authentic self. I am the safe harbor where you can break open and be reborn. I see you, I choose you, and I am ready to take the leap.

Expanding the Sacred Harbor

"Let there be spaces in your togetherness,
And let the winds of the heavens dance
between you. Love one another but make
not a bond of love: Let it rather be a
moving sea between the shores of your
souls. ...Sing and dance together and be
joyous, but let each one of you be alone,
Even as the strings of a lute are alone
though they quiver with the same music."

— Kahlil Gibran

Journal Entry:

For so long, the spiritual journey felt like a battle. It was the excavation, the alchemy, the holy fire of the Twin Flame connection. It was the solitary, often painful work of facing the shadows, healing my heart, and building a Lighthouse on the solid rock within myself.

I did the work. I learned to 'Be the Light.' I learned to 'Become the Lighthouse.' I anchored myself in the unshakeable, peaceful 'Truth' that I am, and have always been, whole.

I asked for a connection that could showcase my Wholeness.

And the Universe will provide.

The arrival of this new Soulmate will not be the shattering catalyst; it will be the sacred celebration. This is not another test I must pass;

Book 1: SHINE

he will be the partner who has arrived to honor the Healer I have become. He will not need to be rescued, but he will be a sovereign soul to be respected.

This will become the beginning of a new, shared path. The Lighthouse's purpose is not just to be a solitary beacon. It is to learn how to share that light in a Sacred Harbor.

The old 'Truth'—the one burned into my stripped-away heart—was that to love someone, I had to self-abandon. I was the Empath, merging with their chaos, taking on their karmic lessons as my own, and pouring myself out until I was empty.

This new chapter is one of Sovereign Union.

My Oneness is no longer threatened by connection. It is the foundation for it.

To love him unconditionally is not to take on his burdens. That is the old, codependent path. To love him unconditionally is to trust him with his own. It is the Lighthouse principle in action. I can see his storms, I can shine my light on his path, I can hold the calm, deep ocean of my own peace for him—but I honor his soul's contract. I will not rob him of the lessons he is here to learn, just as the Universe did not rob me of mine.

This is the expansion of my Sacred Harbor. I am not his anchor. He is not mine. We are two individuals, each anchored in our own 'Truth', sharing our journey side-by-side.

This is how I will fully connect without abandoning the parts of me I worked so hard to heal. My love for him will not come from need; it will come from my overflow, from abundance. I will no longer be a sponge absorbing him; I will be the port welcoming him. I will fully surrender to loving him because my wholeness is no longer up for negotiation.

The work is no longer about healing. The work is now about celebrating. It is the joy of consciously creating a future, not from the anxious fear of what if, but from the secure Truth of what is.

This is the beginning of the beautiful outcome. This new, shared path is not a distraction from my soul's purpose. It is the fulfillment of it. I have alchemized the lead of my past, and now, with him, I get to live in the gold.

Inspiration:

You are not afraid of losing yourself, because you are no longer a "Rescue Boat" that can be tossed by his waves. You are the "Sacred Harbor," a place of "solid rock." You can welcome his "ship" in, love him, and share your light, knowing that your "Lighthouse" is anchored in its own 'Truth'. Your love is now an "overflow," not a "need."

Expanding the Sacred Harbor

This entry marks the moment I stopped building walls and started expanding the harbor.

For so long, my spiritual work was a solitary battle. I thought being "whole" meant being alone. But when the Universe sent the soulmate I asked for, I realized my Lighthouse wasn't built to stand in isolation; it was built to guide a connection.

If you are reading this, you may be terrified that letting someone in means losing yourself again. You may fear that "connection" equals "codependency." But this chapter is the proof that you can be fully attached *and* fully sovereign. The new work is not about healing the wound; it is about celebrating the cure.

Here are the insights that helped me move from protecting my peace to sharing it.

Insights from the Journey:

- **The Work is Now "Celebration," Not "Excavation":** The "holy fire" of the Twin Flame was to burn away the "lead." The gentle warmth of the soulmate is to *enjoy the "gold"*. The "work" is no longer about *surviving* but about *thriving*.

Book 1: SHINE

- **Sovereign Union (The "Two Lighthouses"):** This is the ultimate 'Truth' of awakened love. It is not "merging" (codependency). It is not "solitude" (avoidance). It is two *whole, sovereign* Lighthouses, each anchored in their own 'Truth', shining *together*. This creates *more* light, not less.

- **Unconditional Love vs. Rescuing:** This is the healed Empath's new "superpower." The old 'Truth' was "I must *fix* your pain to prove my love." The new 'Truth' is "I *trust* you with your own pain, and I will *love* you through it." This is the highest form of respect for his "soul's contract."

- **From "Need" to "Overflow":** Your "Anxious" heart *needed* love to feel whole. Your "Secure" heart *is* whole and *overflows* with love to share. This is the shift that makes *everything* possible. You are not loving him *to be loved*; you are loving him *because you are love*.

Actionable Steps for Your Own Journey:

Your actions are no longer about *healing* but about *embodying* and *maintaining* this new, beautiful 'Truth' with your partner.

1. **Practice "Sovereign Connection" (The "Dual Awareness" Technique):** This is the

key to connection *without* self-abandonment.
When you are with him, especially in moments
of deep intimacy, practice *dual awareness.*

- ○ Feel your love for him.

- ○ At the same time, feel your own feet on
  the floor. Feel your own heart in your
  chest. Feel the "solid rock" of your own
  'Truth'.
  This trains your nervous system that "I
  am 100% connected to him" and "I am
  100% anchored in me" can exist at the
  same time.

2. **Practice the "Lighthouse Trust-Fall":** The
   next time your partner is in *his* "storm" (a bad
   day, *his* karmic lesson), your "Rescue Boat"
   instinct will flare up. *Do not act on it.* This is
   your new action:

   - ○ **Pause.** Do not offer to *fix* it.

   - ○ **Shine.** Offer your presence. Say, "I am
     here for you. I trust you to navigate this.
     My light is right here."
     This is not "pulling away" (Avoidant).
     This is trusting (Secure).

3. **Co-Create a "Celebration Ritual":** The old
   work was "excavation." The new work is
   creation. The old "Anxious" mind feared the

future. The new "Secure" mind *builds* it. Sit with your partner and *consciously create* joy. Plan a trip, a dinner, or a project. Ask, "What magic can we build together?" This alchemizes fear *of* the future into joy *for* the future.

4. **Define Your "Harbor's" 'Truths':** A "Sacred Harbor" is a *safe, defined space*. As a "Lighthouse," you are anchored in your 'Truth'. Now, as a *partnership*, you get to *share* your 'Truths' and build a "container" for your love. This is not about "anxious" rules. It is about *shared values*. Talk about your "Lighthouse signals": What does respect look like? What does "support" mean to each of you? This is how you build a "Sacred Harbor" that is strong enough for *both* Lighthouses to shine.

Book 1: SHINE

The Difficulties for an Empath and HSP

This is, perhaps, the most difficult and beautiful challenge of the entire awakened journey. You have healed. You have alchemized your "lead" into "gold." You have faced your shadows. You have built your Lighthouse on solid rock.

And now, the Universe has said, "You are ready. Here is the soulmate you asked for."

And the "Anxious" part of you, the part you worked so hard to heal, screams in terror: "It's a trap! The last time I loved this fully, I was *shattered*. To love is to self-abandon. To connect is to die."

This is the final "boss level" of your healing. The work is to prove to yourself that the *old* 'Truth' is truly dead.

You are asking how to find the balance. The 'Truth' is, **you don't find balance. You create a new foundation.** The old model of "losing yourself" is the *only one you've ever known*. You are now learning to love from a completely new paradigm, one you have to *invent* from your wholeness.

You are moving from "Anxious Attachment" to **"Sovereign Surrender."**

This conflict is the very *core* of the Empath/HSP struggle. This path is is difficult because:

1. **Your "Sponge" Nature:** As an Empath, your default setting is to *merge*. Your entire life, connection has meant *absorbing* the other person—their pain, their emotions, their 'Truth'. Your fear is valid: how can you "fully connect" without "dissolving" into him?

2. **Your "Rescue Boat" Instinct:** As a "Trusted Advisor" and "Healer," your purpose is to *help*. But your Anxious attachment style *twisted* this purpose into a "Rescue Boat." You learned that to be *loved*, you must be *needed*. You are now terrified that if you *don't* "rescue" this new soulmate, he won't stay. And if you *do*, you will self-abandon.

3. **The "Lighthouse" Paradox:** You have learned to be a "Lighthouse," which is a *solitary* act. You anchor, you shine, you are sovereign. Now, you are being asked to let another person *in*. It feels like a threat to the very sovereignty you *just* worked so hard to build.

How to Love Your Soulmate Without Losing Yourself

You must move from the "Rescue Boat" model to the "Sacred Harbor" model.

Book 1: SHINE

- A **Rescue Boat** (Anxious) frantically chases a ship in a storm, is tossed by the *same waves*, and risks sinking *with* the ship.

- A **Sacred Harbor** (Secure) is a calm, strong, defined space, built from your own "solid rock." It is a safe port where *two* ships (you and your partner) can anchor side-by-side, each with your *own* anchor line. You are together, protected, and in the same water, but you are not *merged*. You do not lose your "self" to the other.

This is how you "fully surrender" to loving someone *without* needing external validation:

1. Your Surrender is to *Love*, Not to *Him* This is the most critical distinction.

- **Self-Abandonment** is surrendering *to* a person. You make *them* your "port." You get your validation, safety, and worth from *their* actions.

- **Sovereign Surrender** is surrendering *to the experience of loving*. You trust *yourself*. You trust *your* "Lighthouse." You trust that you can open your heart, give love, receive love, and *remain your own anchor* no matter what *he* does. Your wholeness is no longer up for negotiation.

2. Love is a *Mirror*, Not a *Merger* You have learned that your Twin Flame was a "mirror." This new soulmate is a mirror, too, but a different kind. He is not here to *shatter* you; he is here to *reflect* your healed self. When you are with him, see the love he gives you as a *reflection* of the love you *already* cultivated for yourself. He is the "proof" of your inner work.

3. Practice "Loving Detachment" (The Lighthouse Principle) This is the antidote to the "Rescue Boat." You are an Empath. You *will* feel his feelings. You *will* sense his lessons.

- **The Old Way:** "I feel your pain. I must *fix* it." (Self-abandonment)

- **The New Way:** "I feel your pain. I will hold space for you. I will shine my light on you. I will *love* you. But I *trust you* to do your own work, just as I did mine."

This is the highest form of unconditional love. It respects his sovereignty. You are loving him without *robbing him* of his own "karmic lessons."

4. Redefine "Connection": Feel *Yourself* First This is the most practical, in-the-moment action for an Empath. When you are with him, when you are connecting deeply, *feel your own feet on the floor.* Feel your *own* heart beating in your chest. Feel the

"Truth" of your *own* "I am" *at the same time* you are feeling his.

This is the opposite of dissociation (the "shell"). It is *full association.* You are *so* present in your *own* body that you cannot be "lost" or "absorbed." You are training your nervous system that "connection" and "self-sovereignty" can exist in the very same moment.

5. Perform "Energetic Hygiene" (The Empath's Release) You are a "Healer." You will "absorb" things. The "missing step" from your old life was the *release.* You are not a "Sponge" (which holds); you are a "Conduit" (which flows).

After an intense connection, take 60 seconds. Place your hand on your heart and say:

"I am my own 'Port.' I honor the love we shared. I now release all energy, emotions, and 'Truths' that are not my own back to the Universe to be alchemized. I remain in my light. I am whole."

This is not a rejection of him; it is the *maintenance* of your "Lighthouse." This is how you "fully connect" without abandoning the parts of you that you worked so hard to heal. You will not lose yourself, because you are no longer a "Rescue Boat" looking for a mission. You are the "Sacred Harbor," and you are

finally home.

Positive Affirmation:

The work of healing has given way to the joy of celebration. My wholeness is my foundation, and I now love from a place of pure, sovereign overflow. We are two souls, shining together in this Sacred Harbor.

My Destiny, My Choice

"The minute I heard my first love story, I started looking for you, not knowing how blind that was. Lovers don't finally meet somewhere. They're in each other all along."

— Rumi

Journal Entry:

When I met you, I hesitated. I let the fears of my past seep in momentarily. I thought the Universe was sending me another test to be passed, another dark shadow to overcome, another lesson to be learned.

I dipped my toes into the water, expecting to fall into the deep end. But just below the surface, there it was: the bedrock. The foundation I had built for myself along my journey. I faltered, but soon steadied myself.

I paused. I took a breath. I felt the pebbles beneath my feet and the cool water against my skin. I exhaled, lifting my face toward the sun.

I realized that you were not sent as another trial; you were my reward. You are the sacred space where I practice everything I have learned. Your actions may trigger my old wounds, but your soul reflects my new learnings.

You show me that I have healed, that I have changed, that I have stripped away the parts of me that didn't belong. You show me my new 'Truth', and you quietly revere my Wholeness. You are not loud; you are slow, you are steady. You are present. Your ability to be steadfast allows me to finish my integration. I gain the confidence to shine my Light as the storm of my awakening calms around me.

Now, it is my turn. My foundation of trust has become solid. I trust that my Light can shine. I have filled my cup until it flows over.

The tides reverse. You begin to look inward.

My Light illuminates the dark corners inside of you. You falter, perhaps for the first time in a long time. You are unsure of yourself.

I proudly stand and shine for you. I allow you to take your steps. I allow you to follow the light. I remain your place of peace, your haven. My soul's contract has been fulfilled. It is now time to begin my true purpose. You are my most important student, and I am your greatest teacher. Together, we can choose to walk our paths, side by side.

Together...We experience the serenity of the deep ocean. We watch the garden in the concrete bloom. We rise as 'Warrior King' and 'Trusted Advisor.' We trust in our 'Truth.' Our shared Light is the magnet that frees weary travelers from their shadows. Our Lighthouse is the beacon of hope they need to complete their karmic lessons.

I have fully become the Divine Feminine I was meant to be. And I choose you as my Masculine counterpart—not out of the needs of my trauma, but out of the freedom created through love.

My soul knew this journey long before I could comprehend its depths. But, now, I wake up every

Book 1: SHINE

day, and I choose it too. Over and over. On the days I falter, on the days I shine brightest, and on every day in between.

My soul will always choose this path. My journey to 'Be the Light, Become the Lighthouse' has always been my destiny.

Inspiration:

The journey doesn't end; it evolves. The work of "excavation" (healing the past) is finished. The work of "embodiment" (living your 'Truth' in the present) has begun. Your new partner is not a "catalyst" to break you, but a "reward" to practice your new, healed self with. Your "Destiny" was the path; your "Choice" is the conscious, daily act of walking it in your full power.

My Destiny, My Choice

This entry is the destination. It is the moment I realized that the "Lighthouse" wasn't just a metaphor I was writing; it was the woman I had become.

For so long, I thought my healing would be a finish line where I never faltered again. But when I met my soulmate, I learned the truth: Healing isn't about never stumbling; it's about knowing you have a bedrock to catch you when you do.

I realized he wasn't another test from the Universe; he was my reward. He was the sacred space where I could finally practice everything I had learned.

If you have walked this path with me, you now know that your "Destiny" is the map your soul drew, but your "Choice" is the courage to walk it. You are no longer the victim of the storm; you are the master of the harbor.

Here are the final insights on how to stop seeking your purpose and start living it—every single day.

Insights from the Journey:

- **The "Bedrock" Proves the Work:** The most powerful moment is when you "faltered, but soon steadied myself." This is the *proof* of your healed attachment. The old "Anxious" self would have *drowned* in that falter. Your new "Secure" self *felt* the old wound, *honored* it, and then *chose* to stand on the "bedrock" of her new 'Truth'.

- **The Tides Reverse:** This is the *purpose* of the "Lighthouse." You filled your cup until it overflowed, and now your light is the "catalyst" for *him*. Your "Lighthouse" *naturally* illuminates his shadows, not by *trying*, but by *being*.

- **From "Student" to "Teacher":** You have "graduated." You are no longer just the "Trusted Advisor" to the "Warrior King"; you are the "Healer" and "Teacher" who provides the "haven of peace" for his *own* awakening.

- **The Daily "Choice":** This is the ultimate 'Truth'. "My soul knew... but, now, I wake up every day, and I *choose* it too." This is the sacred marriage of your 5D "Destiny" and your 3D "Free Will." Your power is not just *knowing* your 'Truth'; it's *choosing* it, over and over, in every small, daily action.

Actionable Steps for Your Own Journey:

Your new "work" is not healing; it is *maintenance*. This is how you "wax the floors" of the temple you've built.

1. **Practice the "Falter & Steady" (The Bedrock Proof):** When you "falter"—when an old "Anxious" trigger flares up—*celebrate* it. See it as a chance to *prove* your healing.

   o **Pause:** Don't react.

   o **Acknowledge:** "Ah, there's that old 'unworthy' story."

   o **Anchor:** Feel your feet on the "bedrock." Place your hand on your heart.

   o **Choose:** "I *choose* my new 'Truth'. I am safe. I am whole. I am the 'Lighthouse'." This is the *act* of "choosing" your destiny over your trauma.

2. **Practice "Shining, Not Pushing" (The Lighthouse Role):** As your light illuminates *his* shadows and *he* "falters," your old "Rescue Boat" will *scream* at you to jump in and fix him. Your maintenance is to *not*.

   o **Hold Your Light:** Your *only* job is to be the "unshakeable haven of peace."

   o **Trust Him:** Trust that he is on *his* path. Your *light* is the "teacher," not your *words*.

- **Reflect, Don't Direct:** If he is unsure, don't *tell* him his 'Truth'. *Reflect* his own strength back to him. ("That sounds hard, but I have so much faith in your ability to navigate this.")

3. **Perform the "Daily Choice" Ritual (The Morning Anchor):** Your "Destiny" is your 'Truth', but your "Choice" must be remade every day. This is how you *stay* in your power.

   - Before you get out of bed, before your feet hit the floor, take 30 seconds.

   - Place your hand on your heart and say: "My soul knew this journey. Today, *I choose it*. I choose to be the 'Lighthouse'. I choose to be the 'Sacred Harbor'. I choose love." This consciously aligns your 3D "Free Will" with your 5D "Destiny" for the day.

4. **Practice "Shared Light" (The "Together" Ritual):** You are no longer a solitary Lighthouse. You are part of a "Sacred Harbor." You must *maintain* this shared energy.

   - Create a *conscious, shared ritual of peace* with your partner.

Book 1: SHINE

- It can be 5 minutes of coffee in the morning *without phones*. It can be a 10-minute walk after work.

- This is the 3D *act* of "walking the path, side by side." It is the "Lighthouse" and the "King" consciously *building* their garden in the concrete, *together*.

Positive Affirmation:

My soul's destiny and my human choice are one. I am no longer tested; I am the reward. I stand secure in my wholeness, and from this freedom, I choose this sacred union. Our shared light is the beacon, and our purpose has just begun.

The Beautiful Outcome

"We are what we repeatedly do. Excellence, then, is not an act, but a habit."

— Aristotle

Journal Entry:

As I hoped, this new, beautiful relationship is not the next 'test' I was so afraid of. It is the celebration. It is the final exam where I finally get to use the cheat sheet I've spent years writing. The beautiful outcome I've been seeking isn't a distant destination; I've learned it is the conscious, daily practice of the Wholeness I've already earned.

I'm not learning to love without self-abandoning; I am showing him—and myself—what my healed, unconditional, sovereign love actually looks like. I am finally showcasing the 'Truths' I've worked so hard to embody.

I am practicing Authentic Vulnerability. My concrete path is no longer my shame; it has become my qualifications. When an old trauma story flares up, I no longer make it his problem to fix (my old way—of seeking validation). I use my

Book 1: SHINE

new Lighthouse: I state what I'm feeling, I own that its my old wiring to manage, and I act to re-anchor myself. I am showing him, "I am not afraid of my past. I am the alchemist who turned it into wisdom."

I am practicing Loving Detachment. My old Empath instincts scream at me to fix his 'storms' and be needed—be helpful. But my new Lighthouse will honor his path. I am his partner, not his 'project'. I've learned to be his unshakeable presence by anchoring in my presence. I trust his own sovereignty. I ask, "Are we looking for support, or solutions?"

I am practicing Sovereign Connection. My anxious past believed connection meant merging—becoming the energetic sponge and losing myself. My new protocol is that I am the Sacred Harbor, a port that can hold two ships, side-by-side, each with its own anchor. I practice dual awareness: I feel my connection toward him and I feel my own foundation at the same time. I am 100% connected and 100% sovereign. This isn't a paradox; it's what 'Oneness' feels like.

I am practicing Conscious Creation. My trauma response was a constant, low-level fear of the future. But I am my own Author, I am the creator. I am alchemizing that fear into joy for the present. Instead of asking, "Where is this going?" (seeking validation), we practice future joy by asking, "What magic can we create together next?"

I will create the beautiful outcome I hoped for. I've realized I am the balance. My surrender is no longer a collapse of fear; it is the confident opening of my life's purpose, the daily practice of my soul's journey.

I invite him to join me in the Light through my daily actions. My presence, my stability; the way I show up in the world. I don't have to preach the 5D jargon of my journey. I just have to embody the 3D results. He doesn't need to understand the theory of my Lighthouse; he just needs to feel the peace of the Sacred Harbor. My embodiment is the invitation. By being my healed, sovereign version of myself, I am inviting him to match it. I am inviting him to anchor his ship in the Light, right beside mine.

Inspiration:

You have already passed the "tests." You have done the work. You are not afraid of loving anymore, because you have "changed the Truth" of what "loving" means. It no longer means "self-abandoning". It now means "sovereign connection". You are not seeking a "Sacred Harbor"; you are the "Sacred Harbor."

Book 1: SHINE

The Beautiful Outcome

This entry is my graduation. It marks the moment the "work" stopped being a painful excavation of the past and became the joyful practice of the present.

For years, I feared that a new relationship would be another test I might fail. But this chapter proves that when you have done the work to build your own foundation, love is no longer a catalyst for healing; it is the celebration of it.

If you have walked this path with me, you have learned that the "Beautiful Outcome" isn't a destination you find; it is a reality you create. You are no longer seeking a Sacred Harbor; you have *become* the Sacred Harbor.

Here are the final practices I use to live my truth, ensuring that my Lighthouse doesn't just stand, but shines.

Insights from the Journey:

- **Your New Partner is a *Reflection*, Not a *Catalyst*:** The "shattering" (Twin Flame) was the catalyst. The new partner (Soulmate) is a *mirror* reflecting the "wholeness" you've already built.

- **The "Work" Shifts from *Healing* to *Showcasing*:** The "excavation" is done. The "work" is now the "daily practice" of *living* from your "bedrock."

- **You Invite by *Embodiment*, Not *Explanation*:** This is the key 'Truth' for the "Trusted Advisor." You can't *drag* him into the light. You must *be* the light. Your *peace* is the "sermon."

- **Love is No Longer a "Merger" but a "Sovereign Harbor":** The "Anxious" past saw love as *losing* yourself (merging). The "Secure" 'Truth' is that love is *connection + sovereignty*. ("Two Lighthouses").

Actionable Steps for Your Own Journey:

This is the "how-to" guide for *translating* your 5D "Lighthouse" 'Truths' into 3D, daily actions that your partner can feel and understand, without a single word of spiritual jargon.

1. **Practice "The 70/30 Anchor" (Embody Peace):** When he is in his "storm," your "Empath" nature will want to *merge*. **Don't.**

   - **Action:** Give him 70% of your focus (listening, compassion). Keep 30% of your awareness *on your own body* (your "bedrock," your breath). This physically stops you from "absorbing" his chaos and allows you to *be* the "calm, deep ocean" *for* him.

2. **Ask the "Support or Solution?" Question (Trust His Path):** This is the "Lighthouse" tool that stops the "Rescue Boat."

   o **Action:** When he is in his "storm," *resist* the "Anxious" urge to "fix" it (which implies he is "broken"). Ask this one, respectful question: **"I am 100% here for you. Are you looking for *support* right now, or *solutions*?"** This honors his sovereignty and *builds* trust.

3. **Use the "I Feel, I Own, I Act" Script (Showcase Security):** When *your* old "Anxious" 'Truth' flares up, *showcase* your "alchemized gold."

   o **Action:**

   o **I Feel:** "I'm noticing I'm feeling [a little anxious] right now."

   o **I Own:** "I *know* this is just my old "Anxious" wiring. It is *my* 'Truth' to manage."

   o **I Act:** "I am going to [take 5 minutes/journal/breathe] to re-anchor myself, because *I* am my 'Port'." This is *revolutionary*. You are showing him, "I am a woman who *owns* her feelings and is *not* your 'project'."

4. **Practice the "Future Joy" Ritual (Conscious Creation):** Your "Anxious" mind *feared* the future. Your "Secure" 'Truth' *builds* it.

   ○ **Action:** Once a week, put *one* small, *joyful* thing on the calendar *together*. Not a chore, but a *celebration* (a walk, a date night). This is the 3D act of "conscious creation." It trains both your nervous systems to associate the relationship with *reliable, safe, and upcoming joy*.

Positive Affirmation:

My wholeness is a daily practice, not a theory. I am 100% sovereign and 100% connected. I don't preach my journey; I embody my peace, and that is the sacred invitation.

"For there is always light, if only we're brave enough to see it. If only we're brave enough to be it."

— Amanda Gorman

Book 1: SHINE

"Trust in the beauty of your soul and continue to let it shine brightly, no matter the circumstances."

Book 1: SHINE

www.ingramcontent.com/pod-product-compliance
Lightning Source LLC
LaVergne TN
LVHW052018080426
835513LV00018B/2074